M A

T A R A

PRAIRIE PLAY SERIES NO. 34

MATARA

The Elephant Play

CONNI MASSING

NeWest Press

Library and Archives Canada Cataloguing in Publication
Title: Matara : the elephant play / Conni Massing.
Names: Massing, Conni L. (Conni Louise), 1958– author.
Identifiers: Canadiana (print) 2023015347X | Canadiana (ebook) 2023015350X | ISBN 9781774390825 (softcover) | ISBN 9781774390832 (EPUB)
Classification: LCC PS8576.A7973 M37 2023 | DDC C812/.54 — dc23

NeWest Press wishes to acknowledge that the land on which we operate is Treaty 6 territory and a traditional meeting ground and home for many Indigenous Peoples, including Cree, Saulteaux, Niitsitapi (Blackfoot), Métis, and Nakota Sioux.

Editor for the Press: Anne Nothof
Cover and interior design: Natalie Olsen, Kisscut Design
Cover photos: Aflo Co., Ltd. / Alamy Stock Photo, Adehoidar / Shutterstock
Author photo: Ken Christie
Production photos: Marc J. Chalifoux
Series: Prairie Play Series No. 34

| Canada Council for the Arts | Conseil des Arts du Canada | Funded by the Government of Canada / Financé par le gouvernement du Canada | Canada |

| accessCOPYRIGHT FOUNDATION | Alberta Government | Alberta Foundation for the Arts | Edmonton | edmonton arts council |

NeWest Press acknowledges the support of the Canada Council for the Arts, the Alberta Foundation for the Arts, and the Edmonton Arts Council for support of our publishing program. We acknowledge the financial support of the Government of Canada through the Canada Book Fund for our publishing activities.

NeWest Press
#201, 8540-109 Street
Edmonton, Alberta T6G 1E6
www.newestpress.com

No bison were harmed in the making of this book.
Printed and bound in Canada

For Lucy

MARC J. CHALIFOUX

Production History
Matara premiered at Workshop West Playwrights Theatre,
November 28 – December 9, 2018.

Cast and Crew
KAREN Elinor Holt
MARCEL Minister Faust
ROMNEY Patricia Zentilli

DIRECTOR/DRAMATURG Tracy Carroll
SET, LIGHTING, COSTUME AND PROJECTIONS T. Erin Gruber
PROPS DESIGNER AND BUILDER Randall Fraser
SOUND DESIGN Darrin Hagen and Nick Samoil
STAGE MANAGER Steph Link
APPRENTICE STAGE MANAGER Steven Sobolewski
PRODUCTION DRAMATURG Mukonzi Musyoki

Characters
KAREN female, forties
MARCEL thirty-five, a Rwandan immigrant
ROMNEY female, mid-thirties

A Guide to the Punctuation

...   wherever it occurs in a line, means the thought is, for whatever reason, incomplete.

--   means the thought is intended to continue. It may be cut off or it may be picked up by another speaker but the thought continues.

—   means a new thought interrupts the existing thought, often indicating a change of direction within a sentence and/or the speaker's mind.

/   placed between two words in a sentence means the next speaker interrupts the line at this point so that, for a time, the two characters are speaking simultaneously

Setting

The action takes place in and around a mid-sized urban zoo.

PROLOGUE

Darkness. The sounds of a zoo coming to life. A whistling call.
Silence. Some chattering which builds into a chorus, only to
be superseded by the roar of a big cat. More birdcall. Hoots,
chipchipcharoo. Call and response. Nickering and snorting.
The bass rumble of an elephant.

KAREN enters, dressed in a zoo keeper's uniform.

MATARA appears in the half-light, on the other side of the stage.
She's a 35-year-old Asian elephant represented on stage as an
impressionistic video image and/or puppet. MATARA trumpets.

KAREN: Matara...?

A long moment. Retreating into the dream.

> We're on a walk — through the river valley — but
> it's dark...

> The trees are shining, shedding light on the path.
> Or is that the moon? (*beat*) I don't know where
> we're going but we're in a hurry.

We hear an elephant trumpeting, layered on top of the sounds
of the other zoo animals.

> We walk and walk along the valley that was
> carved out during the ice ages for our...
> procession. Down to the water. To the river.

The trumpeting grows in volume. KAREN clocks MATARA's
distress. Slightly more urgency in the following.

There's the boat — the river boat ark. With monkeys and lemurs and yaks and — there's Becky. And Juba and Jakarta and — everyone's nervous and chittery — chattery. Derek the large snowy owl sits on the highest point of the boat. The sky is getting pink — we have to hurry — we push off. Down the river... to the ocean?

Mattie?

The cacophony of animal noises stops suddenly. The dream has ended abruptly, interrupted by...

ROMNEY: (*offstage*) Hello?

Scene 1: Elephant House

KAREN stands by MATARA, peering into her face. ROMNEY has entered the elephant house, teetering on high heels or wearing something else fairly inappropriate for this environment.

ROMNEY: Karen?

A beat, then:

KAREN: Yeah.

ROMNEY: My name's Romney. I've been hired by the zoo to do a little consulting. In light of the recent debacle.

KAREN: Debacle?

ROMNEY: The death of your male elephant... (*checks her phone*) Cheerio?

An awkward pause.

So of course I wanted to meet you and Nelly.

KAREN: Matara.

ROMNEY: Ma-ta-ra?

KAREN: It means magnificent creation.

ROMNEY: I'm confused.

KAREN: She has two names. Because visitors to the zoo are always calling out to her. "Nelly — look over here! Over here!" Like that. We don't want her to be distracted by contradictory commands so she has a public name and a private name.

ROMNEY: Got it. Well I think I'll refer to her as Nelly if you don't mind.

KAREN: (*with a shrug*) Okay.

ROMNEY looks up at MATARA.

ROMNEY: So...this is what all the fuss is about.

Scene 2: Elephant House

Sounds of a large group of excited children entering the space. KAREN waits for them to settle then...

KAREN: Good afternoon and welcome to the elephant talk. My name is Karen and this is Nelly.

Nelly is an Asian elephant and she has lived here at the zoo for most of her life. I have known Nelly for most of my life, too, because the first time I came to the zoo I was...(*pointing to someone in the audience*) about your age...and Nelly had just arrived.

Elephant facts. Nelly has a very flexible and powerful tool in the form of a trunk. She can tear down a tree or pick up a blade of grass with this handy dandy thing. Elephants are among the very few species who can recognize themselves in the mirror.

The commands to MATARA are embedded in a phrase.

(*to MATARA*) And you're quite the beauty isn't that right?

KAREN stares at MATARA expectantly. After a few seconds
MATARA nods her head.

> My job is to keep Nelly healthy. She has exercise
> and enrichment every day to challenge her mind
> and keep her fit. For instance, sometimes I hide
> her food so she has to work a little bit harder to
> find it. Sometimes we do crafts, although Nelly
> isn't very good at origami, are you? (*No response
> from MATARA*) Hey—not so hot at the needlepoint
> or the origami, are you? (*After a few beats MATARA
> finally shakes her head*) Nelly likes classical
> music, peppermint and Picasso. (*KAREN smiles
> at the response of the "elephant talk" audience*) It's
> true—Nelly is a connoisseur of modern art and
> she also likes to make abstract paintings.

*We hear, faintly at first, the sounds of a protest, a crowd of
people chanting. KAREN clocks this.*

> Any questions? (*listens for a moment*) Nelly sleeps
> over there in the other end of her house. She
> braces herself against that big soft pile of sand.
> See? It makes it easier to get up in the morning.
> (*listening*) She is a vegetarian but she's been
> known to eat plastic. So—thanks for coming to
> see Nelly and now...yes? (*listening, a long beat*)
> Yeah, there used to be another elephant. We were
> all very sad when Cheerio died. (*another question*)
> Of course Nelly misses him—we all do.

*The sounds of the protest fade up and out. The elephant talk
audience is gone.*

> (*to MATARA*) How you doin'? Hey...

KAREN peers into MATARA's face.

Scene 3: Marcel's Security Shack

MARCEL makes an entry in his logbook.

MARCEL: May 6th. Notified maintenance about lights outside east barn. A quiet night. But this morning...the protesters from Wildwatch are gathered outside the zoo again. At first their leader, Jeremiah, addresses me as "Dude." I say that he is free to call me this as long as I may refer to him as "exalted of the Lord." Jeremiah is confused by this as he evidently does not know the biblical meaning of his own name. Now he calls me Marcel or simply "Hey."

Scene 4: Parking Lot

MARCEL approaches KAREN.

KAREN: Hi...

MARCEL: Good morning, Karen.

KAREN: You're...it's Marcel, right?

MARCEL: Yes. I wanted to let you know...I am finding the Wildwatch pamphlets everywhere. The protesters are very concerned about elephants but not very worried about trees.

MARCEL hands a pamphlet to KAREN.

KAREN: (*reading*) "*Nirvana Elephant Sanctuary: a refuge for aged, ailing and abused elephants. Eighty-five elephants...*" some of them are from Sri Lanka, like Matara.

MARCEL: In truth I do respect the passion of this group. They are here each day in the morning when I leave and they are still here when I come back. All the time pleading for Nelly — Matara — to be sent to a place where she will have the company of other elephants —

KAREN: This is her home and we are her family!

MARCEL: I did not mean to upset you. (*beat*) I tried to get Jeremiah and the others to move off the property last night but they feel entitled to be here.

KAREN: To collect signatures for their petition —

MARCEL: And to call for the closure of all zoos.

KAREN: Are you kidding? They have no idea what they're talking about! Seeing wild animals in a zoo was pretty much the most important thing that happened to me as a kid. It changed my life! If it weren't for the zoo I never would have seen a wild animal. Well except for deer and coyotes. And a moose, once. Most kids will never have the chance to go on a safari but they can come right here and see a tiger or a lion or an elephant. A real live *elephant*. I will never, ever forget the first time I saw Matara...

MARCEL: I imagine it was —

KAREN: These animals are ambassadors for their species! How else will the people who see them learn to care about animals so that they will stand up for the ones who are being driven out of their homes by industry or climate change or war?

An awkward silence.

MARCEL: I do not know.

KAREN: Sorry. I didn't mean to —

MARCEL: No. It is good to know what you think.

KAREN: I'm not totally against protests. I mean, normally.
I think they keep us honest and besides, sometimes it forces the city to give the zoo more
money for things the animals need. But these
guys — they don't understand. Matara's still getting
over losing Cheerio — it's only been a couple of
weeks — and she doesn't need all this...attention.

MARCEL: I understand.

MARCEL starts to leave.

KAREN: Hey, you go to university, right? When you're
not here?

MARCEL: Yes.

KAREN: How's that going?

MARCEL: Ahh...I will say that I've discovered that thinking
about my thesis is not the same as actually
writing it.

KAREN: (*amused*) Guess not.

MARCEL: And I still haven't admitted to my very kind
adviser that I am more interested in my English
literature course than in environmental engineering. I am meant to be useful when I go home.

KAREN: Right. Well... have a good sleep.

MARCEL: Thank you.

KAREN exits. MARCEL remains, staring off.

>Vincent? Vincent, was that you — standing with the protesters? Not a funny joke.

Scene 5

ROMNEY gives a speech to the zoo staff.

ROMNEY: Good morning. My name is Romney Millard. I'm a corporate narrative coach with a background in strategic community outreach and fundraising facilitation. I am here to change the public's perception of this zoo. In the aftermath of Cheerio dying and the unfortunate incident with the harbour seals, the word out there seems to be: this is a place where animals do not thrive. Obviously we need to create a different story. And who is the audience for that story? The public, by which I really mean the parents of the huge number of children who attend our programs and visit the animals. And then there's the media — who will help us if we help them. And the protesters: a small but vocal contingent of Wildwatch disciples who are not likely to engage with our message. I plan to work with the communications director, obviously — but also all of you who work directly with the animals — in order to create a brand new forward-looking vision. Thank you.

ROMNEY exits.

Scene 6: By the River

MARCEL: May 13th. A new English word: blizzard.

MATARA and KAREN walk, meet MARCEL.

       Snow in May! Will it never end?

KAREN: Eventually.

MARCEL: I thought the seasons were meant to be guidelines for when to expect grass and flowers as opposed to—

KAREN: Sorry. The only month we haven't had snow here is...

MARCEL: June? (*KAREN shakes her head*) July?

KAREN nods, grins.

MARCEL: Such a vision before me: an artificial palm tree bent sideways from the weight of snow. An elephant from sunny Sri Lanka standing in front of a curtain of misting sleet.

KAREN: It'll melt by tomorrow. For sure.

MARCEL: You have restored my faith.

KAREN: Thought you'd be long gone by now.

MARCEL: Not quite yet. Lately it has been my habit to sit by the river at the end of my shift. I put my worries and cares in a small boat and send it downstream. Normally the river whispers and sighs but after the spring storms and the endless rain that has followed the river is too busy to stop and talk.

MATARA takes a few steps away.

KAREN: Whatcha doing, Mattie? You going down to the
         river, too?

MARCEL: They said on the news there is a boat downstream
         from here — a floating restaurant —

KAREN: Oh yeah, I think I knew that.

MARCEL: Noah's ark — with prime rib. The owners are
         having financial trouble. In the summer they
         serve food and have live music — in the winter
         they can't make any money because the boat is
         frozen in place.

KAREN: In the winter we're all frozen in place.

MARCEL: Yes...

MARCEL moves off.

Scene 7: Elephant House Office

KAREN: Matara's breathing sounds worse and she
         wouldn't eat this morning. I found Cheerio's old
         blanket and gave it to her. I think she likes that.
         (*beat*) Last night I dreamed about...Noah's ark?
         Matara and I went for a walk down to the river —
         we got on the riverboat and floated away.

         And then I woke up.

Scene 8

ROMNEY rehearses, reading from her notes. She records herself on her phone.

ROMNEY: Good morning, children! I have an exciting
announcement. (*another try*) Hey! Hey kids...

ROMNEY replays a few words, grimaces, tries again.

Hey kids! Write a poem about your favourite zoo
animal — (*tries out a few animal noises*) — and win
a prize! A great big...prize. (*stalled*) I am... itchy
all over.

Scene 9 Parking Lot

MARCEL: I come up from my river walk and there is Jeremiah,
delivering a speech to a reporter and a television
camera. He is speaking — rather poetically — about
the dread season ahead. But it's almost summer,
says the reporter. Jeremiah says that "winter is
always coming" — and when it does, there will be
"no spongy jungle moss under the elephant's feet,
just snow and concrete." I must confess, I feel
I can relate. Jeremiah finishes his performance —
he embraces one of his acolytes — he is excited
about the number of signatures he has collected
for his petition to have Matara taken from the zoo.
I am walking across the parking lot to the bus stop
when I see that Karen has been ambushed.

KAREN: (*to JEREMIAH*) She has lived here practically all
her life! We're the only family she's ever known!

MARCEL: (*to JEREMIAH*) Jeremiah. If you harass a staff member again, other than myself, I will call the police.

KAREN and MARCEL watch JEREMIAH leave.

KAREN: Did you see him roll his eyes?

MARCEL: I did.

KAREN: I wanted to punch him.

ROMNEY charges up.

ROMNEY: (*to KAREN*) What have I told you about engaging with the protesters —

KAREN: I wasn't "engaging" — whatever that means.

ROMNEY: Just — don't.

KAREN moves off. MARCEL starts to follow.

(*to MARCEL*) Hello?

MARCEL: I beg your pardon?

ROMNEY: It's just — I thought I'd met everyone on staff.

MARCEL: My name is Marcel. I work the night shift. On security.

ROMNEY: I'm Romney — great to meet you.

MARCEL: Yes. Thank you.

ROMNEY: I'm new — obviously.

MARCEL: Ah, yes—

ROMNEY: Ten days in and I have no idea…I've met most
of the animal keepers. Complete freaks who
clearly prefer the company of toads and lizards
to human beings. And God help me if I interrupt
the shit-shoveling to ask anyone a question.
(*beat*) How long have you worked here?

MARCEL: Nearly six months.

ROMNEY: Ah. And are you from…Africa?

MARCEL: Yes. More specifically / from Rwanda—

ROMNEY: What brings you to Canada?

MARCEL: Not the climate.

MARCEL moves off.

Scene 10: Zoo Grounds

*KAREN and MATARA begin a lumbering walk through the zoo.
We hear animal noises and see shadows or silhouettes
representing the animals.*

KAREN: Mattie? Come on, we'll visit the zebras.

They walk a little further and stop to see the zebras.

Jakarta…Juba, look who's here.

*KAREN peers up at MATARA as if expecting her to say some-
thing but MATARA is unresponsive. They continue walking.*

KAREN: Here we are at the ocean, eh? Waves crashing
          and shiny seals climbing up on the rocks.

KAREN's radio squawks.

ROMNEY: (*on her radio*) I'd like to speak to Karen, please.

KAREN: (*on her radio*) Karen here.

ROMNEY: Is that Karen?

KAREN: Yes.

ROMNEY: Where's Nelly?

KAREN: She's off display.

ROMNEY: I have a family here that's hoping to see her.

KAREN: Tell them to go and see the new tree frog exhibit.

ROMNEY: Where are you?

KAREN: We're on a walk.

ROMNEY: One of these folks is a potential donor who would
        like to buy one of Nelly's paintings. I think that's
        worth ten minutes of—

KAREN: (*turns off her radio, turns to* MATARA) Romney
          says she's been researching elephants—I think
          that means she's been watching videos on
          YouTube.

*MATARA makes a sound. KAREN laughs but then watches as
MATARA sways from side to side.*

KAREN: Come on. We can say hello to the hippopotamus,
          the elk, bison, yaks, red kangaroo, red-necked
          wallaby, two-toed sloth.

KAREN peers into MATARA's face, as if waiting for a response.
MATARA is silent.

          (*a soothing sing-song*) Giant anteaters, black-
          and-white ruffed lemurs, ring-tailed lemurs,
          black-tailed prairie dogs, Siberian tigers, Arctic
          foxes, brown bears, grizzly bears, polar bears,
          wolverines, and miniature donkeys. Donkeys!

Still no response from MATARA.

          Mom says that's my party trick but it feels more
          like carrying the whole zoo around in my head.

          She's gone to Machu Picchu. I gave her a list
          of birds she should look out for. She gave me
          a list, too.

          Number one: Have more relationships with
          humans. I asked her if she had someone in
          particular in mind? Number two: Get rid of
          the fire-bellied toads in my bedroom. Number
          two is probably connected to number one.
          But she knew about me fostering animals
          when she moved in.

MATARA stops, refusing to go on with the walk.

KAREN: Look, here's your favourite camel. Hello, Becky...
          Mattie? Say hello to Becky?

MATARA sways from side to side. Perhaps we hear her laboured
breathing.

KAREN: Romney told me about an elephant in Korea who mimics human speech. What would you say if you could mimic Romney?

MATARA is unresponsive.

KAREN: I'm worried about you. What is it, my love? Is it Cheerio?

KAREN caresses Matara's eye area or rubs her tongue.

Mattie...?

Scene 11: Zoo Grounds

MARCEL: May 23rd. No Wildwatch today. Is it possible they have given up?

ROMNEY: I've always loved giving people bad news.

MARCEL: On the contrary —

ROMNEY: Well someone has to do it, right?

MARCEL: Wildwatch has gone to City Hall.

MARCEL moves off. ROMNEY approaches KAREN.

ROMNEY: Karen? Do you have a minute?

KAREN: Not really. Matara's done with her foot soak and I have to go —

ROMNEY: Wait. Wildwatch presented their petition to city council today — and city council agreed to have the elephant examined. *(no response from KAREN)* Examined by a special veterinarian consultant in order to determine whether she is well enough to be moved to a sanctuary. In a warm climate. Like Nirvana.

KAREN stares at ROMNEY, stunned.

KAREN: No...

ROMNEY: I'm really sorry but it's true. Are you okay? And I imagine you heard about Clementine. The gibbon?

KAREN walks away.

ROMNEY: Karen? Great talking to you, as usual.

ROMNEY spots MARCEL.

Hey...Marcel!

MARCEL enters.

MARCEL: Yes?

ROMNEY: Just starting your shift?

MARCEL: Yes. And you are...working late?

ROMNEY: Yeah. I just spent the whole day tête-à-tête with communications finding a way to create a positive context for the news about Clementine. *(MARCEL looks puzzled)* She died. *(MARCEL nods)* Do you have any questions about...that?

MARCEL: Is this really part of your job?

ROMNEY: Well as you can imagine, this is terrible timing. I mean, we're in the middle of this controversy about our elephant and then our one and only gibbon pops off.

MARCEL: Extremely inconsiderate. So. What is the "positive context"? For the death?

ROMNEY: Oh. Well, I mean it's the circle of life, right?

MARCEL: Ahh—such good news for my loved ones that their sudden death closed a loop.

ROMNEY: I'm sorry—did someone just die? I mean / shit, sorry—

MARCEL: It is not necessary to—

ROMNEY: Let me try that again. May I offer my condolences?

MARCEL: (*nods*) Thank you.

MARCEL starts to walk away.

ROMNEY: (*calling after MARCEL*) Hey, I'm doing a presentation to a bunch of managers from an oil company Friday morning and I'd love to have your feedback.

MARCEL: I'm afraid I don't understand...why.

ROMNEY: Well I'll be talking about wild animals and I just thought—with you being from Africa—you might have a perspective. A unique perspective.

MARCEL: Thank you for the invitation. However, I will not be at work that day.

MARCEL exits. ROMNEY stares after him for a moment.
We hear the sound of a nearby animal, perhaps the huffing
of a big cat.

ROMNEY: What are you looking at?

Scene 12: Elephant House

MATARA stands by herself, swaying from side to side.
KAREN enters and watches for a moment. MATARA spots
KAREN and responds somehow, reaching out with her trunk?

KAREN: Mattie...I had another weird dream about you.
You were...somewhere else. On a beach? Near a
jungle? I can't really remember but I think I was
right there with you.

KAREN pulls a tool out of her pocket.

How is my lovely chum today? (*a command*) Foot.
(*leans in and examines a foot*) I'm going to trim off
this little bit. Jim'll get you a treat. (*begins to work*)
Oh, that looks a bit tender. (*another command*)
Down. Good girl. (*A gentle pat or stroke*) Hey
Brenda, wanna prep the foot soak?

MATARA sways from side to side. KAREN lays her hands gently
on Matara's flank.

KAREN: Are you dancing? Is that a waltz? No, it's not.
You're...

A beat.

KAREN: I have to admit—something the Wildwatch guy said stuck with me. He kept saying "Who speaks for the elephant? How do you know what *she* wants?" (*a beat, peering into MATARA's face*) Please tell me what you want. So I can speak for you. .

KAREN leans into MATARA and closes her eyes.

Scene 13: Zoo Grounds

Sounds of the zoo shutting down for the night. MARCEL does his night patrol.

MARCEL: The Arctic fox. During the day he runs around and around and around on a track so it is good to see him rest now. (*a beat*) I wish you would rest, Vincent.

You know, when we were in convent school, one of the nuns who knew of our rather traumatic past used to pat me on the arm and say "*try not to dwell on it.*" Really? You and I huddled together in the banana grove watching the end of the world? I have tried to forget. And yet here we are.

Continues walking. Stops in front of another enclosure.

Derek, the large snowy owl. I stare. He stares back. We are both under surveillance. I believe the floodlights around the zoo are a torment to the owls at night—in the wild they would have total darkness. But of course I have no opinions.

MARCEL: The American eagle sleeps on a perch in his cage — ah, but the zoos no longer call them cages. They are enclosures. Habitats.

(*listening to VINCENT*)

Yes, I see that his feathers are straggly and dull. But his wing has been amputated so he would be dead if he hadn't been rescued.

In another space, KAREN peers at MATARA on a WEBCAM.

KAREN   Mattie — you're still awake.

MATARA sways from side to side.

KAREN: Why don't you try to sleep?

MARCEL: Now we will visit Sasha...tiger, tiger burning bright.

KAREN: You could go somewhere nice in your dreams. To the beach — and the hot, steamy jungle.

MARCEL: Sometimes I see his yellow eyes, wide open and glowering, like Derek's.

He is another who would likely be dead by now in the wild. Hunting, being hunted, ranging across the mountain passes and barren steppes of Eastern Russia. Instead here he is — in his diorama — suffering from insomnia. Like me — and you. (*peering in at SASHA*) Try not to dwell on it.

KAREN: I'm sorry — I have to sleep. Good night, my love.

KAREN exits.

MARCEL: Most people I meet here believe that death is the very worst thing that can happen. I suppose you would agree.

Scene 14

KAREN: (*in the elephant house*) The last round of antibiotics didn't work. I can tell Doc is worried — though she doesn't think it's the same infection Cheerio had. I say maybe the vet consultant will have some ideas about that. Doc says he'll be here Friday. I tell her about Matara's swaying from side to side because I know that kind of stereotypic behaviour is sometimes a sign of stress. Or even mental illness — at least in humans.

MARCEL: (*by the river*) The mountain streams have rushed down to add their voices to the river.

KAREN: Doc Clara gets a bit crusty with me and says Matara is probably just missing the stimulation provided by another elephant. So Jim and Brenda and I have another meeting about her enrichment program.

MARCEL: When I ask about the rising water I am told it is the "spring runoff." No one is concerned.

KAREN: Jim and I help the vet consultant examine her.

ROMNEY: (*in her office*) I immediately start to panic.

KAREN: The results of the examination won't be available for at least ten days.

ROMNEY: Without an elephant…

31

KAREN: (*to MATARA*) Of course I want the vet to say you're healthy enough to travel. At least I think I do. But the truth is...

ROMNEY: Ringling Brothers went out of business after they lost their elephants!

KAREN: You are my whole world. And I am yours...

Scene 15

ROMNEY addresses a school group.

ROMNEY: Thank you for all your fantastic entries to the zoo's poetry contest!

KAREN brings a watermelon into MATARA's enclosure.

KAREN: Hello my lovely chum.

ROMNEY: (*reading*) "Remember Me" by Ashley Froman
Is it true that elephants never forget?
I know I will never forget seeing Nelly today
So big and gentle and maybe her flappy ears
heard my whisper
Nelly is beautiful!

KAREN: Look what Jim brought for you. Watermelon!

KAREN sets up the watermelon so MATARA can stomp on it.

Go crazy.

ROMNEY: Good job, Ashley! And what do we have here?
(*reading*) If Nelly could talk I think she would tell
us a joke
About elephants in the room…

MATARA ignores the watermelon, sways from side to side.

KAREN: Come on, you can do it.

ROMNEY: (*reading*) I like the art Nelly makes
She paints the sunrise and sunset
Does she see that by our river?
Or remember a hotter sun from Sri Lanka

KAREN: Bananas?

KAREN offers MATARA a couple of bananas.

Trunk up. Up!

*MATARA curls a banana up with her trunk and throws it over
KAREN's head.*

Mattie!

MATARA picks up the second banana and eats it.

ROMNEY: Aha — what's this?
(*reading*) Swinging through the trees
Or should I say monkey bars
Monkey business is cool!

KAREN: Good girl. (*calling out*) Brenda — wanna bring
her ball?

ROMNEY: Is that supposed to be a haiku?

KAREN: (*peers into MATARA's face*) I know you'd rather play ball with Cheerio but I'll do my best, okay? (*a beat*) Okay?

KAREN leans in, closes her eyes, listens.

ROMNEY: (*reading*) "Sad Elephant" by Jessica Smith
All the rivers of Asia and Africa are traced on her skin...
Routes for trade of salt and silk and spices
And places for tears to run...

ROMNEY crumples up this entry as she exits. KAREN steps away from MATARA.

KAREN: Darkness and sad shapes floating in water? No...words.

(*pulling paper out of her pocket*) One of the kids gave this to me yesterday — to read to you.

(*reading*) "The First Annual Blow My Big Top Circus." By Jennifer D.
It happens in a meadow. There will be stations or booths where kids can eat ice cream and the animals can eat bugs or small frozen rodents like they find tasty. There will be no fences or cages. At the end I will call all the animals back to the main tent and if they don't come back...they don't come back.

Scene 16

In the darkness, the sound of rain, building steadily to a downpour and then slowly fading out.

Scene 17

MARCEL deals with protesters.

MARCEL: Yes—Jeremiah—I understand you are celebrating. But you must deconstruct this campsite!

MATARA stands in front of an easel. KAREN sets up small buckets of paint and brushes. KAREN isn't thrilled to be doing this and neither is MATARA.

KAREN: (*to the audience for the painting session*) Hello! Guess we'll get started with the painting. I hand brushes to Nelly and she decides what colours she wants to use.

MARCEL: I will give you one hour.

ROMNEY makes a presentation.

ROMNEY: Good morning. Welcome to "perspectives on nature," a very special executive team-building exercise, designed with Alconbridge Oil in mind. As Horace Walpole said in 1777, "Alas! We are ridiculous animals."

MARCEL: (*to JEREMIAH*) You know, my friend—this dynamic between humans and animals will never completely disappear.

MATARA wields a brush with her trunk, then hands it back to KAREN.

KAREN: Nelly normally prefers blues and greens. But today...

ROMNEY: What can we learn from our friends in the animal kingdom?

MARCEL: (*to JEREMIAH*) The original zoos were royal menageries. The lions and tigers kept in the Tower of London reflected the status of the monarch.

ROMNEY: One of the things we admire the most is their ability to act on pure instinct. To make and execute powerfully unambiguous decisions as they hunt — and are hunted.

MARCEL: No. "Dude" is not "on side" with you.

ROMNEY: Anyway, imagine you are in the jungle and it is deepest darkest night...

MARCEL: I have no opinion, just an academic interest.

ROMNEY: You hear the scream of a howler monkey and you are unperturbed.

MARCEL: There are many accounts of human zoos...

ROMNEY: The monkey is not a threat. Although they do reek.

MARCEL: ...a practice of displaying captive foreigners which began during the Renaissance...

KAREN hands MATARA a brush and she puts a couple of paint strokes on the canvas.

ROMNEY: Actually this whole zoo has the most unbelievable pong.

KAREN hands MATARA another brush but MATARA hands it back to her.

MARCEL: I said, during the Renaissance —

KAREN: I think the painting may be done.

MARCEL: Never mind.

KAREN: Nelly loves having her tongue rubbed as a reward for all her hard work.

KAREN rubs MATARA's tongue.

                    (to MATARA) Hey, what's up?

MATARA kicks over a bucket of paint or knocks down the easel. KAREN moves off with MATARA.

KAREN: Romney wants you to do more paintings for some fundraiser the zoo's having.

ROMNEY: Something else I've noticed since I started this job: animals are not afraid to look us in the eye. With no subtext or shyness or judgement.

KAREN and MATARA walk. MATARA stops. KAREN peers into her face.

KAREN: I look into your eyes and I get so much back. I've always had trouble looking humans in the eye. But that doesn't mean I won't stand up for you. How about this: from now on you don't have to do anything you don't want to do. Okay?

I totally trust Doc Clara but maybe this vet consultant will have some ideas about your mood. I just want — everyone just wants the best for you.

Scene 18: By the River

MARCEL stares at the river. He's whispering to someone or something. KAREN approaches, watches him for a few moments until he stops mouthing words and closes his eyes.

KAREN: Marcel?

MARCEL: Ah...good morning.

KAREN: Sorry to interrupt.

MARCEL: May I help you?

KAREN: Did you happen to check in on Matara last night?

MARCEL: I always do.

KAREN: She was still awake at one when I looked at her on the webcam. At least I think she was.

MARCEL: Yes.

KAREN: And later — was she...?

MARCEL: Sometimes it's difficult to say if she is resting because I know elephants can sleep standing up. Much like myself.

KAREN: Elephants don't sleep a lot at the best of times but I can tell from the imprints in Matara's sand bed that she's restless. I'm worried she might be having nightmares. (*beat*) Every night when I leave I say "sweet dreams."

MARCEL: And does she answer you?

KAREN: She used to. (*beat*) You were probably joking.
I have to learn not to take everything so literally.

MARCEL: I often have the same problem.

KAREN: Matara has a great sense of humour — she's really
mischievous. At least she used to be. These days...

MARCEL nods sympathetically.

You probably think I sound crazy.

MARCEL: Not at all. I know animals can communicate; it must
be frustrating for them that we do not understand.

KAREN: I *do* understand. I've always talked to animals.
I was about twelve the first time an animal
answered me back. In colours and pictures,
nothing like human words. But then I didn't really
feel human anyway. (*a beat*) I don't know how to
explain it, only sometimes I wondered if I was an
alien brought down to earth. I just couldn't figure
out why I'd been sent. Until I met Matara.

MARCEL: Matara is very fortunate to be in your care.

KAREN: Oh no — I'm the lucky one.

An awkward silence.

But ever since Cheerio died, she's been... silent.
I've tried everything but she's just not responding.
(*beat*) Please don't tell anyone that I think I can
talk to animals.

MARCEL: As long as you do not report on my conversations
with...the river.

KAREN smiles, moves off.

Scene 19: Marcel's Security Shack

MARCEL: Romney wants me to view the recording of the presentation she made to a group of oil company executives. She says she wants my opinion. Experience has taught me that when people say this they merely want you to confirm their bias.

ROMNEY: (*as she enters*) I think it went very well. What did you think?

MARCEL: Your audience seemed to be attentive. Especially the alpha dog who asked all the questions as a way of displaying his own knowledge.

ROMNEY: Oh him—that's Benson. Mr. Oakes. A *very* big player. So…?

After a beat…

MARCEL: I wasn't certain about the point of the presentation.

ROMNEY: I'm trying to raise the profile of the zoo in the business community, so that they'll see us as a resource.

MARCEL: I mean the content of your speech. That we should emphasize our wild instincts while asking the animals to forget theirs? And also, in the context of the zoo. Where animals are less and less wild. Where their natural instincts are subjugated, suppressed.

ROMNEY: We all have to suppress our natural instincts, don't we? Or maybe not.

MARCEL: But if an instinct is irrepressible, what happens when you are no longer permitted to act on it?

ROMNEY: Hey, did you notice that I used the word "atavistic" in my presentation? I thought you'd appreciate that, after telling me the other day that I was—

MARCEL: When I saw you in front of the snow leopards—

ROMNEY: Oh that—

MARCEL: I believe you were hissing—

ROMNEY: It's just a thing I do at the beginning of the work day. Like...go team.

MARCEL: I see.

ROMNEY: Do you really think that I have "a tendency to return to an animal condition"? Perhaps you meant to use another word...

MARCEL: Feral?

ROMNEY: Very funny. More like...frantic.

MARCEL: Busy?

ROMNEY: Probably my own fault. (*beat*) The rule in my business is "under-promise, over-deliver." I'll confess I may have made a miscalculation in this case. I just told the zoo I'd make a major announcement at the time of the summer solstice gala—less than three weeks from now. I just don't know what the hell it's going to be.

MARCEL: May I ask you a question?

ROMNEY: Fire away.

MARCEL: What are you doing here? Working at the zoo.

ROMNEY: My last job ended…rather abruptly. I needed the gig.

MARCEL: I understand. But…

ROMNEY: I do actually have a little background working with animals. When I worked at the opera they did a production of *Aida*.

MARCEL: *Aida*…

ROMNEY: The director wanted an elephant. He had to settle for a cheetah. A tame, farting cheetah.

MARCEL laughs.

The whole thing was a nightmare.

MARCEL: I'm sorry — I was amused by the idea of wild animals as actors. Though I suppose the zoo is a kind of theatre as well. The animals are posed in their scenarios. There are set pieces — the palm tree in the background of the monkey enclosure, meant to represent all of the Amazon jungle. The white molded plaster in the fox enclosure: a snowbank in the high Arctic. Both the audience and the animals are asked to suspend their disbelief.

An awkward pause.

ROMNEY: It's weird but you make me nervous.

MARCEL: I…make you nervous.

ROMNEY: I mean I'm usually pretty comfortable around men.

MARCEL: For my part, I am still getting used to the women in this country.

ROMNEY: And how's that going?

MARCEL: I will let you know.

MARCEL starts to leave.

ROMNEY: Have a great night off—catching up on your sleep?

MARCEL: I confess I can no longer sleep when it's dark, even when I'm not working. It's an old habit.

ROMNEY: Insomnia?

MARCEL: No—vigilance.

ROMNEY: Ha. Sweet dreams.

MARCEL and ROMNEY move off in different directions.

MARCEL: (*stops to listen to Vincent*) Yes, my brother—I am being gently mauled before a big cat makes a meal out of me.

ROMNEY: Feral? Either he has the best deadpan delivery I've ever heard or he really meant—no, he was definitely flirting with me. All that talk about instincts…yum.

Scene 20

KAREN: (*in the elephant house office*) I meet with Doc Clara and suggest maybe we could cancel the elephant talks for a few days. I'm worried that it will be obvious to anyone who sees Matara that she isn't herself. And also—I don't want her to feel any extra pressure.

ROMNEY records a journal entry on her phone.

ROMNEY: Almost every single kid who has entered the contest has written their poem about Nelly. It's not exactly a blinding epiphany to conclude it's all about the elephant.

KAREN: Doc says that Matara's condition has improved a bit since her last checkup and that the zoo never wants to send the message that we can't meet the needs of our animals. Especially while we're waiting for the verdict from the vet consultant. I'm confused by this. I wish I was better at understanding...politics. But I wouldn't know where to start. I say what I mean. So do the animals.

ROMNEY: (*recording on phone*) I am starting to have some very strange feelings about my own place in the food chain. In the animal kingdom. For instance, irrepressible instincts. I think I can speak to that. I feel...wild? I mean, more than usual.

Scene 21: Elephant House / Admin Office

ROMNEY is in her office looking at the webcam on her phone and talking to KAREN on the radio. We may also see the webcam view of MATARA and KAREN.

ROMNEY: So how's Nelly doing on her weight loss program, Karen?

KAREN: She's losing weight because she's not eating.

ROMNEY: Would you mind elaborating just a little bit for me and the guest I have here with me? What kind of plan is Nelly following, anyway? Low-carb? High protein? The Paleo diet?

KAREN: She's not eating because she's lost her appetite.

ROMNEY: Don't I *wish* I'd lose my appetite! Ahh, here we are. The weigh-in. Drum roll, please...

We see MATARA step on to a scale (on the webcam).

ROMNEY: Last time, she weighed 8600 pounds. That was down 150 pounds from her previous all-time high! Let's see how she's doing now — what's the good news, Karen?

The webcam view suddenly disappears.

The webcam's crapped out!

KAREN: I'm not sure it's such a great idea to publicize the weigh-ins anymore.

ROMNEY: Why? I know for a fact that the vet recommended she be put on a diet.

KAREN: That was months ago. And that's when the communications director started doing these monthly...sideshows. But now she's losing more weight than we want her to.

ROMNEY: Okay. Shit.

KAREN: I will try to get them to fix the webcam though — I like to check in on Mattie after I get home at night.

ROMNEY: Do you mind if I pop over there and shoot a little video on my phone of her stepping on and off the scale?

ROMNEY charges off. We shift focus to the elephant house.

KAREN: Actually we're pretty busy right now…Romney? (*to MATARA*) Wanna go for a walk, Mattie? We'll go for a walk.

ROMNEY runs in, smartphone in hand.

ROMNEY: Could you get her to step on the scale again?

KAREN: I think we're done for now. I'm not going to weigh her again until tomorrow.

ROMNEY: Fine. Guess I'll just tweet out some numbers. Down 175 pounds — whoot. Happy face.

KAREN: What kind of tweet will you send out if Matara is sent to the sanctuary?

ROMNEY: That will happen over my dead body. How can we call ourselves a zoo if we don't have an elephant?

KAREN: Is that a real question?

ROMNEY: Yes! She's our number one attraction!

KAREN: I told the vet I wanted her off display for a few days.

ROMNEY: I know. And the problem is, I see those as competing narratives —

KAREN: What does that mean?

ROMNEY: Our animals are healthy and happy versus...not.
Well, and don't forget it's all eyes on the zoo right
now too.

KAREN: That's a lot of pressure.

ROMNEY: Tell me about it.

KAREN: I meant for Matara — she's not feeling good.

ROMNEY: (*reading from her phone*) Just listen to this.
"Poor Nelly" by Simone Mackey
Is Nelly sick? She looks so old.
If she dies will she be buried at the zoo?
What if it's winter and the ground is frozen?

This is what I'm dealing with.

KAREN: The kids love her, they're worried about her.

ROMNEY: Which is why we need to capitalize on the good
news stories at the zoo — species conservation,
the new meerkat babies, the zebra romance.
I don't think the zoo should be apologizing for
who they are. In fact, I don't think it would be
a bad thing to get more animals. I mean I'm
not talking frogs and snakes here — I mean like
penguins. Or panda bears. Or —

KAREN: The zoo can't even afford to take care of the
animals we have!

ROMNEY: Part of my job is / to raise money for that —

KAREN: -- the city's always nickel-and-diming us on every
little thing —

ROMNEY: I said: I'll find the dough — that's why we're
          having a gala fundraiser —

KAREN: Some of it's not even expensive. Just little things
          we need to make life better for the animals.

ROMNEY: Are you even listening to me? My job is —

KAREN: My job is to protect Matara —

ROMNEY: Yes of course but —

KAREN: I've been bitten by a lemur, a snake, a gibbon,
          sprayed by skunks and snubbed by every kind of
          cat. But I've never been betrayed or abandoned
          or disappointed by an animal.

ROMNEY: Good for you —

KAREN: I am disappointed by the way the zoo is handling
          this. And Matara.

ROMNEY: Look. Officially I have never been told that
          the elephant is too sick to be the focus of my
          programming.

KAREN: *I* am telling you!

ROMNEY: Okay, okay. (*after a beat*) I just want to get a photo
          of her —

KAREN: Careful — / better stay back —

ROMNEY: — to post on the website —

*ROMNEY starts to frame a photo of MATARA with her phone.
MATARA bats the phone out of her hand.*

ROMNEY: My phone! What the hell was that—can you get…?

KAREN picks up the phone and hands it to ROMNEY.

KAREN: She doesn't like the way you smell.

ROMNEY: Seriously, would it be such a bad thing if this whole zoo smelled less like manure and more like Chanel N°5?

KAREN: Yup.

ROMNEY moves off, then stops in front of an animal's enclosure.

ROMNEY: Oh hello…Darwin. Darrell?

We hear the soft hooting of an owl.

I confess I have been over-doing it on the perfume a little because I can't stand the smell of the zoo. Or…of my own body.

DEREK hoots again.

Stop staring at me—it's creepy.

Scene 22: Parking Lot

It is raining lightly but steadily. MARCEL and KAREN meet in the parking lot, close to the river.

KAREN: Hey…

MARCEL: (*nodding*) Karen.

A little awkward silence.

MARCEL: How is Matara?

KAREN: Not good. Maybe elephants never forget but they usually move on. Matara isn't. Moving on.

MARCEL: Perhaps she just has too much time to think.

KAREN: We do enrichment activities with her every minute of the day! She gets exercise — she plays games — she solves puzzles to find her food —

MARCEL: It was not intended as a criticism.

KAREN: Sorry. I'm just — tired.

MARCEL: I only meant to say: in the wild animals do not have time to be depressed. If you do not live in the moment and stay vigilant you will be killed. But the animals here at the zoo have all the time in the world to...ruminate. To grieve?

KAREN: Matara saw her mother killed when she was a baby — in Sri Lanka. And now Cheerio. She wasn't right there when he died but she knew...

MARCEL: Of course.

KAREN: Do you... have too much time to think? I mean — being here alone at night. It must be...

MARCEL: I was a child when the rest of my family was killed. But my brother Vincent died just three months ago. His was the only death I was not forced to witness — so now I see him everywhere.

KAREN: Your brother — was he —

MARCEL: I think his death may have reanimated the memories of my family. So perhaps Matara...

KAREN: Is remembering her mother — and Cheerio.
           I wonder if an animal can have post-traumatic
           stress.

MARCEL: I do not know...why not.

A silence.

           Can you hear the water rushing? I have been
           studying the "spring runoff" instead of my thesis
           proposal. Apparently the river is higher than it
           has been in fifty years.

KAREN: Yeah, I heard on the news that the river boat
           might not be able to get under the bridge.

MARCEL: Some say the rising is cyclical and others say it is
           our own fault that the river is raging. I find I can't
           help but take this personally. I could have plied
           my skills as an insomniac in an office building or
           a mall. But I took the job here so I could visit the
           river and feel connected to a living thing that is
           surging toward its home. And I thought it would
           allow me the time to work on my thesis.

KAREN: Makes sense.

MARCEL: Ahh yes — in theory. Except that I find I have
           nothing to say. I'm meant to submit a preliminary
           draft by the middle of June or I will owe another
           year of tuition. Needless to say I can't afford this.
           And if I don't continue with my studies I know I
           will be sent home.

A beat.

KAREN: I'm sorry.

MARCEL: It is...reality.

KAREN: The vet consultant's report was supposed to be released tomorrow but it's been postponed. I don't know whether that's good news or bad.

MARCEL: What will you do if Matara is sent away?

KAREN: I'll go with her! (*a beat*) Or — I don't know.

MARCEL: Good night, Karen.

MARCEL nods, starts to walk away. Then:

KAREN: I need to ask a favour. The webcam is broken so I can't check in on Matara. I would like to try spending the night with her. Just, you know, sleeping on a cot in the office, so I could hear if...

MARCEL: Your presence will not be noted in my log book.

KAREN: Thank you. Good luck with your studying.

MARCEL: I won't get much done tonight. Wildwatch has built another bonfire.

Scene 23: Elephant House Office

KAREN: I found a doctor, a special kind of vet, who goes into zoos and treats animals for mental illness. I send an email to the director of the zoo — and Doc Clara — with the link to this guy's website. He lives in California. I say that I think Matara might have post-traumatic stress disorder. Doc Clara will probably flip but I have to try. And I have to sleep.

Scene 24: Elephant House

MATARA sways from side to side, makes some sort of noise. KAREN enters, half-asleep.

KAREN: Mattie...?

KAREN strokes MATARA.

> I had the dream about you again, about us.
>
> We went for a walk down to the river — then we just kept going.

MATARA makes some sort of noise in response.

> I put Cheerio's blanket over your shoulders so you'd be warm...because it was nighttime.
>
> We were calm — it was peaceful — even though I think we were running away. To...the riverboat ark. Crazy.

MATARA nudges KAREN with her trunk.

> We got on the boat and floated away to the... mangos? (*bewildered*) What?

Scene 25: Elephant House

KAREN is with MATARA. ROMNEY approaches.

ROMNEY: Do you ever bloody well check your email?

KAREN: Not really.

ROMNEY: It would be terrifically helpful if you could —

KAREN: Is it about the vet's report?

ROMNEY: There's no word yet but the director thinks he's going to sanction moving Nelly. No, I asked you a question about the poetry contest.

MATARA lifts up her trunk or takes a step toward ROMNEY.

Aaah! Is she going to —

KAREN: Better stay back — she really doesn't like —

ROMNEY: I know, I know. So as I said before, most of the poems were about Nelly. And they're not exactly great art but —

KAREN: I could write a poem about the time she pushed Jim's truck out of a snowbank.

ROMNEY: Great — only the poem's supposed to be written by a kid.

KAREN: I was sort of joking.

ROMNEY: And how in the world would I know that?

KAREN: Matara really did push the truck out of the snow.

ROMNEY: Amazing. So — it seems perfectly reasonable to me that a child who writes a heartfelt poetic tribute to Nelly could have a brief but completely thrilling ride on her back as a prize.

KAREN: No. No way.

ROMNEY: The ride could be one bloody minute long. And it would be a hell of a photo op.

KAREN: I said no.

ROMNEY: Or how about the kid gets to take a selfie with the elephant?

KAREN just looks at ROMNEY.

> Look. I am trying to get out ahead of the vet's report with a little positive press. I mean, no matter what he says it's going to be controversial. Right?

KAREN doesn't respond.

> So...the guys from the papers are coming today to get photos, to advertise the gala. Excuse me for having a creative idea but I thought the elephant could wear one of those Venetian masks — for like, five seconds.

KAREN: Why don't you put the mask on one of the goats in the petting zoo —

ROMNEY: Seriously?

KAREN: — or wear it yourself.

They simmer for a few seconds.

ROMNEY: Look. Karen. You and I got off on the wrong foot —

KAREN: Is that what you call it?

ROMNEY: And I know we're all on edge about the verdict from the vet consultant. But in the meantime it would be really great if we could cooperate — collaborate...

KAREN moves off.

ROMNEY: Just—come back here! (*to herself*) It's like talking
to a stick.

KAREN: (*off*) I heard that.

ROMNEY: Good!

Scene 26

ROMNEY: (*in her office*) Wildwatch has convinced Billy Bob
Baxter, the former child star, to voice his support
for their protest. Good old Billy Bob did an
interview in *Entertainment Weekly* and said he
was willing to pony up for the cost of moving our
elephant south.

KAREN: (*in the elephant house*) Romney suggests I watch
a clip of this guy talking in case anyone asks me
about it.

ROMNEY: It's brilliant really—just in case the zoo says
they couldn't possibly afford to move an
elephant, Mr. Baxter will step up.

KAREN: He obviously has no idea what's involved with
moving an animal as big and intelligent as you.

MARCEL: (*by the river*) June 6th. The river is…I would like
to report to you about the river.

ROMNEY: I'm a genius. Well, I actually get the idea from
Billy Bob what's—his—nuts. His making the
grand gesture to finance the elephant "rescue."

KAREN: Mom is back from Machu Picchu. She sees the dark circles under my eyes and says I look like a depressed raccoon. We argue about that and the fact that I haven't done anything on "the list."

MARCEL: I would invite you to — would you please come and listen to the water?

ROMNEY: I need a major donor — someone who can afford to get us another high profile acquisition. I know lots of people don't even want us to have one elephant, never mind two. But I think it would be good for the zoo to have a back-up elephant. I mean a contingency plan. Whatever.

MARCEL: Or, if you would prefer, I can provide you with statistics.

KAREN: I practically have to sneak out of the house to come and be with you.

ROMNEY: I call Benson Oakes, who says his staff is "still buzzing" about the team-building session. Turns out he's mad for elephants and, honestly, a bit mad for me, too. He buys twenty tickets to the gala!

KAREN: And now I can only sleep — and dream — when I'm in the elephant house. (*beat*) Usually the dream gets all mixed up and ends before we make it across the ocean. But last night we got to a patch of jungle with soupy soft air and sunshine. And we never came back.

Scene 27

*ROMNEY talks to a group of kids. KAREN stands nearby with
MATARA.*

ROMNEY: Thanks to all of you for submitting your
wonderful poems to the poetry contest. We had
entries from across the city and it was a really
hard decision for the jury. But today we're so very
pleased to share the winning poem: "Naming the
Elephant" by Lily Spencer. (*acknowledging the kids'
reaction*) Yes—congratulations, Lily. As a prize,
Lily will get to spend some one-on-one time with
(*checks her notes*) Gary, our two-toed sloth. Yay!
And now—the poem.
There once was an elephant called Nelly. Not
Babar, not Dumbo not Jelly-Belly. She eats lots
of hay—and she's here to stay. To play every day
with her pals at the zoo—and us too!

ROMNEY moves off.

KAREN: (*to MATARA*) What did you think of the poem they
read to you? That I'm pretty sure Romney actually
wrote? (*MATARA makes a noise*) Yes, that's what I
thought too.

ROMNEY: (*recording on her phone*) Poetry contest done and
dusted. Massaged the winning entry a tiny bit
because it had this whole riff about Nelly going
away—to Taipei, Malay, Bombay—I didn't think
the poem should promote the idea of her fleeing
to warmer climes.

KAREN: I think we can write a nicer poem for you, huh?
Matara…you are…grey and graceful… (*thinks for
a long moment*)… I just don't have the words.

KAREN strokes MATARA.

> Giant anteaters, black and white ruffed lemurs,
> ring-tailed lemurs, black-tailed prairie dogs,
> Siberian tigers, Arctic foxes, brown bears,
> grizzly bears, polar bears...that's the only poem
> I know.

MATARA makes a noise.

> Wonder if we could fit them all on the ark, huh?

KAREN leans into MATARA, eyes closed for a moment, then steps back, stares at her.

> Birds?

> Lots of birds — because they can find land.

Scene 28

MARCEL: June 9th. The veterinarian consultant has
issued his report saying that travel is not advised
for Matara.

ROMNEY: Fabulous! Full steam ahead to the gala.

KAREN: (*to MATARA*) I spent so much time worrying
about you leaving — now I'm sad you're not
healthy enough to travel. The vet consultant says
your respiratory infection seems to be chronic.
Does that mean...incurable?

MARCEL: Jeremiah and his colleagues are very disappointed. They drown their sorrows with some alcohol — they also nearly drown Jeremiah. I believe the intent was to send a canoe down the river with a burning paper maché elephant. Jeremiah wades into the water to set the fire and is nearly swept away.

I ask for a meeting with the head of the zoo, to warn him about the river and about the increasing desperation of the protesters. He does not return my call.

KAREN: (*to MATARA*) It's weird. Now that I know you are going to be stuck at the zoo I dream non-stop about taking you away.

Scene 29: Romney's Office

MARCEL: Once again, Romney wants my "opinion."

ROMNEY rehearses her gala speech, delivering it to MARCEL. She's well into a bottle of wine. She takes a sip from her glass, launches in.

ROMNEY: Welcome to this year's Summer Solstice Gala. Such a great turnout, blah-blah-blah. So: I have a chart here that will perhaps help you understand our visioning plan going forward.

(*to MARCEL*) You'll have to imagine my brilliant PowerPoint — graphics, photos…

MARCEL: Of course.

ROMNEY: Let's start at the bottom just so you get a sense of—look, of course each and every one of these creatures is just as valuable as the next. (*to MARCEL*) God sees the little sparrow fall and all that. I mean, if you're into that. I'm a Buddhist, I mean I am trying to be a Buddhist, but all that Catholic doctrine was imprinted so strongly with each smack of the ruler from Sister Josephine that even years later...(*back to her speech*) I am trying to forestall your reactions to the sense of hierarchy here in the chart. It has nothing to do with the value of the little lime-coloured gecko versus the Siberian lion.

MARCEL: Tiger.

ROMNEY: Sorry?

MARCEL: The zoo has a Siberian tiger.

ROMNEY: I'll just say "big cats."

MARCEL: They are very different. Lions are much more sociable. Tigers tend to be solitary—

ROMNEY: You know what? You're gorgeous even when you're being sort of pedantic.

MARCEL: Thank you?

ROMNEY: Where was I? (*kicks off her shoes*) Hierarchy— value—gecko...tiger. (*back to her notes*) But it does clearly reflect...the level of interest on the part of the public. The so-called marketability? Yes, I suppose. Surely you can appreciate...that these creatures are less of a draw for the general public than some of the large mammals. Like the giraffes, the hippo and...

*ROMNEY advances on MARCEL in a seductive way, maybe
just invading his personal space? She removes her jacket
and her scarf, tosses them aside as part of punctuating the
following speech.*

ROMNEY: Top of the heap, ladies and gentlemen: Nelly
the Asian elephant. Everyone knows you can't
really call yourself a zoo without an elephant.
And now, I am thrilled to announce that we
may be able to — we most certainly will get —
dolphins — penguins — maybe even a rhinoceros!
That last part is sort of TBA. Thoughts?

MARCEL: You…are a Buddhist?

ROMNEY: Yes! I mean, sort of. But what did you think about…?

MARCEL: I'm sure your audience will be impressed.

ROMNEY: And you…?

MARCEL: It is a very…lively presentation. But now I have
to go check on Matara — and the river.

ROMNEY: (*pouring herself another glass*) Sure you don't want
any wine?

MARCEL: Thank you. No.

ROMNEY rolls her eyes, amused.

ROMNEY: You…are a tough crowd.

MARCEL starts to leave.

Wait. I was wondering…maybe one day this week,
instead of Karen's elephant talk, you could talk
about that gorilla sanctuary in Rwanda.

MARCEL: Perhaps.

ROMNEY: You said you'd been there.

MARCEL: Yes of course but —

ROMNEY: Great.

MARCEL: I also have a favour to ask.

ROMNEY: (*holding up a high heel*) See another one of these anywhere?

MARCEL: Listen — please. I feel that attention must be paid to the river — and to the protesters. Both are rising, rising up. I do not seem to have sufficient status to be considered...to be heard. So I wonder if you could talk to the director of the zoo.

ROMNEY: Sure. No problem.

MARCEL: Thank you. I believe you will have more influence than I, and I also believe it is quite urgent.

ROMNEY: Speaking of my influence...

ROMNEY kisses MARCEL. He backs away.

MARCEL: I'm sorry — I don't wish to pursue this.

ROMNEY: What?

MARCEL: (*handing Romney her scarf*) Your...scarf.

ROMNEY: Fuck you.

MARCEL: Not at this time, thank you —

ROMNEY: If you don't count the time in grade five when I chased Jason Clifford behind the school and he didn't want to kiss me — (*a beat, then:*) You know, I suppose, that I could get your ass fired.

MARCEL laughs.

MARCEL: Oh really?

ROMNEY: I…don't know why I said that.

MARCEL: Perhaps I have given you the idea —

ROMNEY: You didn't — which makes you irresistible. Apparently.

MARCEL: I thought I was better after all these years but I am not.

ROMNEY: You're…sick?

MARCEL: Right now my heart is pounding —

ROMNEY: You're scared of me?

MARCEL: No — not exactly —

ROMNEY: I thought you were just shy but — never mind!

ROMNEY and MARCEL move off in different directions.

My brain is flooded with chemicals. My sweat smells metallic. My breath is rank.

MARCEL: Yes — yes, she is very attractive, Vincent. But nature could not break through. (*listening, then, frustrated*) What do you want me to do?

MARCEL moves off.

Scene 30: Elephant House Office

KAREN: Matara's down another eleven pounds. Her left front foot is tender. I help Doc Clara give her a shot.

I say maybe she's not going to get any better — physically — until she gets over missing Cheerio. I think she needs some other kind of help. Then Doc gives me the news: the zoo is not willing to bring in the specialist — the "animal shrink" — she calls him. She says they can't justify the cost.

So now what? Doc just pats me on the arm. Says she thinks this new drug might do the trick.

As she's packing up her bag she looks around the office. And asks is that your sleeping bag in the corner?

Scene 31

MARCEL: I have five days to finish a draft of my thesis.

KAREN: Three weeks till Romney's contract is done.

ROMNEY: Ten days to the gala.

KAREN: I've cancelled the elephant talks.

MARCEL: Those who have worked at the zoo much longer than me say that every few years there is the threat of a flood, but still they say there is nothing to worry about. No one seems concerned but me.

ROMNEY: Catering, program, transforming the barnyard into a ballroom — all down to me. I even have to supervise the workmen who are putting up strings of little fairy lights all over the zoo.

KAREN: Someone put up lights in Matara's exercise area. They're strung up along the fence and on the big elm tree. I can't wait for this stupid gala to be over.

ROMNEY: On top of everything else I'm pretty sure I'm growing a new tooth. A fang. Right here... The dentist I saw yesterday asked if I was experiencing any unusual stress.

MARCEL: I inform my advisor that I will not be meeting the deadline for my thesis. She reminds me that I will owe more tuition. I remind her that I am already working full-time and sending money home to my aunt and that there is nothing to spare. (*beat*) I tell her about the raging river and my belief that it will soon flow over the banks. A disaster that is...foreseen. I see it, feel it, I *know*. She hands me a tissue. Apparently I am weeping.

Scene 32: Elephant Yard

KAREN: A group of junior high boys come by to watch me walk Matara around her yard. They press into the fence and yell at her. "Hey! Hey you! Do some tricks!" That's the tall one wearing the hockey jersey — he's mad cause there was no elephant talk. I say: this isn't a circus — we don't force Matara to perform. He stuffs some garbage through the fence. One of the other boys — a little guy with a big mouth — has kind of a plastic machine gun — he shoots water into the yard.

Big mouth says to his buddies that he's making a
mud hole for the elephant. Then the little bastard
comes too close. I grab his water gun and point
it back at him. He points his phone at me while
I spray them. You stupid little psychopaths!
Get the hell out! Go!

ROMNEY rushes up.

ROMNEY: What are you doing?

KAREN: My job!

ROMNEY: Really? Because I bet that little scene's gonna end
up on YouTube!

KAREN: So much for empathy —

ROMNEY: What? What are you / talking about?

KAREN: I mean, that's supposed to be part of the zoo's
mission. Once kids see the wild animals, they'll
want to protect them. Those little shits —

ROMNEY: They're kids — and once they tell their parents —

KAREN: Oh get the fuck away from me — from *us!*

ROMNEY: I know you just want the public to go away and
stop bothering your precious elephant —

KAREN: Yes, I do want that / — and she is precious!

ROMNEY: We need the public — and their money — / and yes,
goddamit —

KAREN: Matara's health is the priority —

ROMNEY: — they have to be "entertained"!

KAREN: Is that why you put those stupid lights in her yard?

ROMNEY: The entire zoo will be on display —

KAREN: The workmen left her gate open —

ROMNEY: For five minutes —

KAREN: It's a / good thing Matara didn't get out —

ROMNEY: — because they weren't finished —

KAREN: And I heard you want to set off fireworks at your gala — there is no goddamn way!

ROMNEY: I have tried and tried to collaborate with you, to develop something like a collegial relationship. But I have to tell you — if I wanna set off fireworks — / I will bloody well —

KAREN: The animals will think it is the end of the world!

ROMNEY: It's one night — hardly the apocalypse.

ROMNEY stomps off.

KAREN: (*calling after ROMNEY*) What if it is the end of the world?

Scene 33

MARCEL: June 19th. The protesters are no longer a small ragged band.

ROMNEY: I have a rash all over my body. Maybe I'm allergic to the zoo.

MARCEL: Their numbers have doubled in the last two days.

ROMNEY: Or maybe I'm shedding my skin.

MARCEL: I listen in the darkness beyond their fire. Jeremiah says "This is war!" I am dumbfounded. *This* is war?

KAREN: I write up an official complaint about Romney — the zoo director assures me there will be no fireworks.

MARCEL: Romney?

KAREN: He tries to walk me out of his office.

MARCEL: (*to ROMNEY*) The protesters have a plan for the night of the gala — Jeremiah and his group refer to it as "Project Bigmouth."

ROMNEY: (*dismissive*) Yeah, yeah...

KAREN: But now that I've got his attention I say I want to speak for Matara. I want to rescue her.

ROMNEY: I give Benson a preview of my gala speech. He wants to make the zoo his legacy project!

KAREN: All the animals are talking to me. They know something is coming.

ROMNEY: Benson wants to have a private session with our elephant. Maybe Saturday night after the gala.

MARCEL: Every day more rain. Every day the river rises —

ROMNEY: Benson is going to save the zoo — he is going to save me. (*a beat*) I am developing... there are bumps on my skull that were never there before. Maybe something vestigial...?

Scene 34: Elephant House

KAREN with MATARA.

KAREN: I have been ordered to go home. Management
wants me to "regain my perspective." And get
some sleep.

Of course Jim and Brenda and Amy will take care
of you. They'll feed you and bathe you and take
you for walks. Or...

You and I could go right now — down to the river.
And then just...

Or — I don't know, my love. I just wish...

*KAREN puts her head in her hands. MATARA reaches out to
KAREN and encircles her shoulders with her trunk, then makes
an unusual noise.*

Matara...?

*MATARA lets loose with an ear-splitting trumpet. She repeats
the noise again and again until she is seemingly exhausted.
When she finally stops, KAREN attempts to comfort her,
stroking and whispering.*

Scene 35: Marcel's Security Shack

MARCEL: June 20th. The announcer on the radio sounds
excited when he asks his colleague to "tell us
about some rather apocalyptic weather."

KAREN rushes up.

KAREN: Matara wants to go home!

MARCEL: What?

KAREN: To Sri Lanka.

MARCEL: Where she was born.

KAREN: Yes! And just when I most need to be here they're
         making me take time off.

MARCEL   You have been working too hard.

KAREN: She *is* lonely. She wants to be with other elephants.
         She appreciates everything that we do but...she
         feels very tired. Sad? Maybe just tired. It's hard to
         tell. The pictures, the images are very similar. I've
         noticed how restless she is when I spend the night
         in her enclosure and it's because she's dreaming—

MARCEL: You know it won't be possible to let you in
         tomorrow night.

KAREN: What's—

MARCEL: The gala fundraiser.

KAREN: Maybe you could check on her a little more often
         than usual.

MARCEL: Of course. But you will be able to see her on the
         webcam. It has been repaired.

KAREN: She was born in a teak forest. She remembers how
         tall the trees were. Isn't that amazing?

MARCEL: Yes.

KAREN: I'd love to take her back there—

MARCEL: But surely she isn't well enough.

KAREN: No, of course not. But she dreams about it. (*a beat*) It's been her dream all along and I just didn't understand. (*a beat*) She does remember her mother. And Cheerio. She wonders why she never saw his body after he died. She would like to visit his bones.

MARCEL nods. A beat.

I love her — everyone loves her — but it's not enough.

MARCEL: I'm sorry.

KAREN: What do you think about all this? You never say.

MARCEL: I'm sure it is complicated.

KAREN: You're the only human besides Mom who...never mind, that's stupid. I'm tired, I've started to say things I shouldn't...to you and to Romney and to the director which is why I might lose my job and — please tell me what you think!

A long pause.

MARCEL: I think that it is a good deal of fuss about one creature. I think that the world is full of suffering and I am truly amazed about the focus on a single elephant, beloved though she is.

KAREN: Oh.

MARCEL: This institution is staffed by intelligent, compassionate professionals who care deeply about the animals. But I am not a supporter of zoos.

KAREN: How do you — why do you work here?

MARCEL: The zoo exists. Someone needs to watch over the animals at night. It's an important job.

KAREN: But if you don't —

MARCEL: An important job I'm not sure I will be doing for much longer. It has been a great pleasure working with you, Karen. Getting to know you.

KAREN: Why are you saying goodbye like I'm not going to see you again?

MARCEL: There's a change coming.

KAREN: You're leaving?

MARCEL: I have decided to abandon my thesis. I will study literature and sociology. And anthropology. And history, even though they say it is normally written by the victors. And I will no longer be working here.

KAREN: But won't you still need a job?

MARCEL: The river — the river is going to overflow its banks.

KAREN: I hope not.

MARCEL: I'm sorry but I know this.

KAREN: Every year they say it might flood but it never does —

MARCEL: I am telling you I know! And the animals know, too.

KAREN: What can I do?

MARCEL: Try to make someone listen?

KAREN: No one cares what I think.

MARCEL just nods, pats KAREN on the arm.

MARCEL: I should be looking for my tiger by now. He hides
but I always find him.

Scene 36

KAREN watches MATARA on the webcam.

KAREN: After I get you settled on the ark I go back to
the zoo to get everyone else — and in the crazy
logic of the dream there is room in my van for
the giraffes. Although everyone has agreed to
the plan, they're nervous and chittery-chattery
now that the night has arrived. We have to
hurry. It's almost dawn by the time everyone
has found their place on the boat. Derek the
large snowy owl sits on the highest point of the
cabin on deck and scowls. But I know he'll be
looking out for big rocks and tree trunks in the
water like we agreed. The sky is getting pink as
we push off and start to move down the river
toward the ocean far away...

Scene 37

*Darkness. A whistling call. Silence. Some chattering which
builds into a chorus, only to be superseded by the roar of a
big cat. Silence except for murmuring. More birdcall. Hoots,
chipchipcharoo. Call and response. Nickering and snorting.*

*Sounds of a distant thunder storm and fast-running water
but no sound from* MATARA.

ROMNEY: The night of the gala...

KAREN: Noah's ark was the end of a world, wasn't it?

MARCEL: The stage is set. Each animal posed amidst their
specially designed dioramas.

ROMNEY: Just before people are scheduled to arrive the
rain stops. The zoo looks beautiful. There are
twinkling lights everywhere. Acrobats, jugglers,
magicians — even the catering staff are dressed
in costumes.

KAREN: I can't believe I'm not with you.

MARCEL: Somehow I know the illusion will not hold.

KAREN: For twenty-one years, at least six hours a day,
five days a week, roughly fifty weeks of the year...
I've spent more time with you than most people
have with their own kids.

MARCEL: Project Bigmouth — Jeremiah has arranged for
the television celebrity to be here for the gala.
But his plane is delayed.

KAREN: I know every wrinkle and sound and smell...

ROMNEY: There must be two hundred Wildwatchers outside
the gate. Chanting, drumming, hauling around
that paper maché elephant. I wish a magical
tsunami wave from the river would rise up and
wash them all away.

KAREN: I have tried to think like an elephant. I have tried
to be…an elephant.

ROMNEY: The silent auction raises nearly one hundred
thousand dollars. Plus Benson wants to buy us
some penguins. Or whatever a few million bucks
can buy. I make the announcement and everyone
bursts into applause. And now…

KAREN: Mattie?

ROMNEY: I feel bloody-minded — ruled by instinct. I pinch a
set of keys in anticipation of…

MARCEL: Midnight. As far as I know everyone has gone
home. The rain begins again.

Thunderclaps. A sudden downpour of rain.

ROMNEY: The least I can do is give Benson a little up-
close and personal time. With me. And with the
elephant.

KAREN: I can see you leaning against your sand pile. And I
can *hear* someone talking.

ROMNEY: I am full of champagne and light-headed with
success. I have saved the zoo.

KAREN: Romney? What the hell?

ROMNEY: Things get a little crazy.

MARCEL: I see Romney on the webcam—

KAREN: What is that noise?

MARCEL: —giving someone a tour.

KAREN: Growling?

MARCEL: Or...executive team-building.

KAREN: I'm on my way.

ROMNEY: Wild kingdom!

ROMNEY laughs.

KAREN: It's almost one in the morning when I get to the zoo.

KAREN encounters ROMNEY, who's looking disheveled.

What were you doing in Matara's house?

ROMNEY: You're not even supposed to be on zoo property.

ROMNEY exits.

MARCEL I call the director and tell him: some low-lying
areas of the zoo have started to flood.

KAREN: Matara's gone!

MARCEL: Nature broke through.

KAREN: The gate to her yard is open. Mattie!

*Thunderclaps. A sudden downpour of rain. Sound of rushing
water building and overwhelming the animal sounds.*

MARCEL: The emergency response teams come right
away. We move some animals to higher ground:
the giraffes, the bears, and the older primates.
Many of the protesters come to help.

A collage of panicked animal noises, fragments of voices.
A wave of sound rising and falling. KAREN finds MATARA.

KAREN: There you are — standing in a puddle of cold river
water.

KAREN and MATARA walk slowly from the river toward
Matara's house. While the chaos of the panicked animals is all
around them, they seem to be in a different reality.

You were trying to get to the river and the ark and
the ocean and the place where you were born.

MARCEL: The water is rising in each of the enclosures.
If the animals are not released they will drown.
But if they are freed, they will actually have
access to the river. To swim or be washed away.

KAREN: Are you cold? Mattie?

MARCEL: The elk, moose, deer, zebras, and
donkeys — Jeremiah helps me coax the caribou
into a cattle liner.

KAREN: I don't like the sound of your breathing.

MARCEL: There are harbour seals swimming down the
river. The hippopotamus is crashing against his
gate — he would like to swim in the river, too.

KAREN: There will be a lot of mud tomorrow. You'll like
that, won't you?

MARCEL: The aquariums are too heavy to move — the fish will have to be sacrificed —

KAREN: I'm sorry you're still here —

MARCEL: I help rescue some emus —

KAREN: I'm sorry I couldn't take you home.

MARCEL: I open their cage and I am the one who feels liberated.

Thunderclaps. MATARA stops.

KAREN: That's alright — you love the rain. Come...

MARCEL: They look bewildered but they seem to know: the show is over.

KAREN: It's dark. But the trees are glowing, shedding light on the path. The woods are part of this, they're happy to help. And the moon. She's shining hard from behind those clouds.

MATARA lifts her trunk up toward the sky, then moves again, slowly.

We make our way down to the river and then walk along the valley that was carved out during the ice ages for our journey.

MATARA stops walking.

Yes, my love. Almost there...

MATARA stops, lowers herself to the ground. KAREN crouches beside her.

MARCEL: I release all of the owls into the night. I feel better than I have in some time.

KAREN: We get to the boat just before dawn. Somehow the others are already there, waiting to go.

MARCEL: I will go home once more and visit your bones, Vincent. Then maybe we can both rest.

KAREN: The sky is getting light as the river boat just barely makes it under the bottom of the bridge. Then we're off. Floating. On and on and on...

ROMNEY encounters MARCEL.

ROMNEY: Wow, this is, like — biblical! I knew the river was high but I had no idea —

MARCEL: I told you. And told you. The rain and the runoff from the mountains —

ROMNEY: But it's so sudden —

MARCEL: Not really. There are many very efficient people here helping with the rescue. You can go home —

ROMNEY: Are you kidding? I want to be here —

MARCEL: Because there will be plenty of bad news and you would / like to spread the word —

ROMNEY: Oh, come on — I want to help.

MARCEL: You have already been immortalized.

ROMNEY: What?

MARCEL: Matara's enclosure. The web camera —

ROMNEY: But it's not working —

MARCEL: I made sure it was repaired so that Karen could have her peace of mind.

ROMNEY: I was doing my job!

MARCEL: Really?

ROMNEY: — trying to ensure the future of this zoo.

MARCEL: How is that?

ROMNEY: He wanted to see Matara!

MARCEL: Matara is dying.

A cacophony of natural sounds (animal cries, human voices raised in command or panic) along with inorganic sounds (vehicle engines, media reports). The wave builds, subsides, builds again, like a radio tuning. Then: everything stops.

KAREN strokes MATARA and stares off.

KAREN: Just after we push off and start to move slowly down the river toward the ocean far away, I scratch your lovely big ear flap and whisper. Can you feel the breezes from Sri Lanka? What's that? (*listening*) You say, "I remember it as Ceylon."

You do the most beautiful dance on the deck of the boat. Most people would never dream an elephant could be so light on her feet. Someone somewhere is playing a piano and you spin around very, very slowly.

KAREN: It's sunny and beautiful when we arrive and walk down the ramp to the beach. You pull mangos off the trees. Drink from a waterfall. Then walk into the jungle. I used to dream that I'd go with you.

MATARA is still.

I wish I could tell you...every day when I looked into your eyes...to be in your presence...it was a wonder. (*a long moment*) It was...

There are no words.

Silence.

THE END

MARC J. CHALIFOUX

MY ZOO STORY

BY CONNI MASSING

Please note: although the essay is inspired by my research at the zoo and describes my real experience there, I have chosen to protect the identities of the staff by referring to them with different names.

Never in my wildest dreams did I imagine that my work as a playwright would include wrestling with a reindeer...

I have always loved animals of every sort, from household pets to wild creatures. It had occurred to me more than once to write about this powerful feeling, but I could never seem to find the right "angle." Over time, I got a bit more specific in my musing, zeroing in on the question of our *relationship* with animals, which runs the gamut from passionate caring to mind-blowing cruelty. Some people feel they are uniquely situated or equipped to get inside the heads of the animals, who are deemed to be emotional, intelligent participants in the conversation (animal empaths, so-called "whisperers"). Several times in the last year I've been at a restaurant when someone in the group has passionately declared that they're no longer eating octopus because of recent discoveries about their intelligence. Interesting that it should make a difference. At the other end of the spectrum, there's the widely held societal belief that it's okay to kill animals because it's their destiny to feed us; besides, they're stupid or insensate. And lest I sound sanctimonious, I'm still a carnivore myself. It's complicated.

Around 2012, I become aware of the story of a lone elephant at the Edmonton Valley Zoo: Lucy. Her presence there is hugely controversial. Activists believe the elephant should be with her own species, in a herd. The zoo staff, on the other hand, as well as feeling that Lucy isn't well enough to make a long trip to an elephant sanctuary, believes that they are family to Lucy. Or certainly the only family she's ever known. Finally something clicked for me in terms of a focus for my play: I knew I wanted to explore a relationship between an elephant and an elephant keeper. And soon I had a kind of thesis question I was interested in exploring: What if the most important relationship in your life is with an animal? An animal whom you love and strongly believe you can communicate with but who may not be as fulfilled by the relationship as you are? How tragic for both beings in that relationship.

I tumbled down the rabbit hole of researching and writing and feeling.

I read everything I could find about zoos and watched more than my share of nature documentaries about elephants. I visited the Edmonton Zoo regularly, trying to catch glimpses of Lucy, ghosting around, eavesdropping on other people's conversations about her and the zoo as an institution. And feeling a bit like a spy. I wondered if I looked suspicious, as practically everyone else was accompanied by small children or least a partner. I did indeed get to see Lucy several times, either on one of her walks around the zoo grounds or while she "performed" for large groups of children, but I knew it was absolutely crucial that I interview some of the staff who worked directly with her. However, though zoos are in the business of welcoming visitors, they are also extremely protective of their staff, some of whom receive threats from anti-zoo activists. I made several failed attempts to interview keepers at zoos in either Calgary or Edmonton. The Calgary Zoo had just sent their elephants to a sanctuary. I was desperate to connect with the keepers there who would no doubt be feeling emotional about this, but I suspected this was also the very reason the zoo didn't want me to talk to them. However, the Calgary Zoo turned out to be inspiring in a completely different way. In 2013, the city was devastated by a once-in-a-generation flood and the zoo was particularly hard-hit. I was fascinated by the first-hand accounts of zoo staff desperately trying to save animals during this biblical-style tragedy and filed it away for creative consideration.

Meanwhile, I had started writing the play. I knew I wanted to have an elephant and elephant keeper; I also knew the keeper needed to be in conflict with someone about caring for the elephant. That counterpoint character became a fundraising consultant whose priority was attracting big money to the zoo. The third character, a Rwandan immigrant, was inspired, in part, by a quote from a Zambian government official, Jean Kapata, commenting on the international outrage in the wake of an American big game hunter shooting a lion called Cecil. ("The west seemed more concerned with the welfare of a lion in Zimbabwe than of Africans themselves.") I was happy with the configuration of these three characters, but the actual structure of the story eluded me for months. The only constant in all this was the final moment of the play. The last line of a speech by the central character came to me early on and never changed. It proved to be my anchor throughout the creative process.

During these early days of working on the play, I did manage to interview someone who'd been Lucy's keeper for a number of years—which was great—but I knew it was no substitute for an up close and personal experience with her and the other animals. Then, to my great delight, an opportunity presented itself in the fall of 2015. Edmonton's Workshop West Playwrights' Theatre (WWPT) launched an innovative project which embedded playwrights in the environments of their choice (a funeral home and a university math department, among other locations), in order in inspire short pieces of writing which would later be performed as an evening of theatre. Of course I chose the zoo for my residency and, amazingly, the theatre was able to broker a deal for me to spend several months there.

Our zoo sits on a beautiful piece of land in the North Saskatchewan River valley and it is home to roughly 350 inhabitants from 150 species. First opened in 1959 as Storyland Valley Zoo, it has since shed the amusement park image and rebranded as Edmonton Valley Zoo. Between November, 2015 and March, 2016 I would be allowed to shadow keepers and interview staff there, with the understanding that I would write a short piece inspired by my residency.

The residency informed my writing in countless ways. Many of the discoveries I made there about my attitudes toward animals and the zoo were destined to be background and would never end up in the play, except to the extent that they coloured impressions and feelings. That's as it should be. But all these years on I still seem to have a good deal of pent-up feeling about the zoo—and about Lucy—almost as if writing the play wasn't enough of a catharsis. So here I am. What follows are select journal entries from my time at the zoo, as well as some reflections on how the experience influenced my work-in-progress.

NOVEMBER 12, 2015

First day of the residency. (It's a huge relief to finally be "legit.") I turn up at the appointed time and get the basic orientation from a special events coordinator, who will facilitate connections with the zoo's staff. Of course I'm most interested in the keepers, but the zoo also employs site workers, custodians, administrators, marketing and community outreach specialists, interpreters, box office clerks, and fundraisers. There's also an army of volunteers, who assist the keepers working directly with the animals.

I get some basic instructions about the protocols for being in the presence of animals. Take your cues about noise and distance from the keeper. Always wear the steel-toed rubber boots provided to staff. If I or one of my household pets is sick, I'm to stay home from the zoo, as some viruses can spread from human to animal. I feel another surge of gratitude for this opportunity as I think about the leap of faith they're taking by having me here, allowing me access to this world without knowing if I'll be sensitive enough not to frighten an animal or inadvertently interfere with the keepers' work. And who knows what I'll take it into my head to write about them? (Especially given the ongoing controversy about Lucy's presence.) All in all I'm amazed to be here. But I feel a bit guilty, too. When I'm given a spot on the agenda of a big meeting of the keepers I tell them I'm interested in investigating our relationship with animals — and that's true — but I don't admit to my obsession with one specific animal...

NOVEMBER 13

My first real shift of this gig and I get to spend it with Lucy!
And, even better, she's going to create some abstract art, one
of the things she's best known for. We gather in the Elephant
House, a cavernous sort of barn that includes a large open
area for Lucy's "performances" and for staging the care she
receives, as well as a set of bleachers for visitors. Her house
also has a sand pile for Lucy to sleep on. I watch as two
keepers — Lucy always has at least two attendants — set up
an easel and prepare some paints.

Lucy is an Asian elephant, rescued from an elephant
orphanage in 1977 and later transported to the Edmonton
Zoo. At the time I started my residency she was forty-one
years old and suffering from a respiratory problem. She's
huge, of course, weighing in at roughly 4000 kilos, though
Asian elephants are not nearly as large, on average, as
African elephants. Still, when you're standing a few feet
away, she is undeniably impressive. I'm learning that this —
standing close to an elephant — is another unique feature of
Edmonton's zoo. In most zoos around the world, elephant
keepers reach through bars into pens or corrals to care for
their charges. Here in Edmonton, though the keepers observe
strict protocols in terms of safety, they are allowed to care
for Lucy with no barriers between them and her.

Today a local artist called Joe Green has been allowed
the privilege of "painting" with Lucy, handing brushes to
her and marveling at her creative choices — she seems to
prefer blues and greens — and watching as she applies bright
splashes of colour to the canvas with her trunk. Joe is in total
awe of Lucy — as am I — and can't help himself from kissing
her trunk when she finishes one of her swoops of colour
and passes the brush back to him. Lucy does seem to enjoy

this activity — or at least the treats she's rewarded with for going along with it — so perhaps that's reason enough to do it. It's also a great way to promote the zoo, and much more pleasant for Lucy than some of the publicity stunts from a bygone era at the zoo. (I saw photos of Lucy being dressed up for Klondike Days, for instance. And the keepers also occasionally rode on her back for a photo op.) If you ever doubted that Lucy is the star attraction of this institution, a visit to the gift shop, with paintings by Lucy, photographs of Lucy, and myriad elephant-themed tchotchkes, would disabuse you of that notion.

It should also be said that this activity (painting) falls under the heading of "enrichment" for Lucy. The keepers also hide treats in odd containers so that Lucy has to figure out a puzzle in order to get them, play games with her, and train her to do simple tricks in response to commands. Zoo staff spends a considerable amount of time creating enrichment activities for all the animals here.

At the end of my shift I can hardly wait to get back to my desk to make notes about my first impressions. I'm very interested in the way the keepers relate to Lucy. (I want the elephant keeper in my play to sound authentic.) When I talk to my pet cats I can't resist a radical upswing in pitch, various nonsensical endearments and repetitive phrases. (Who's a good boy? Who's a good boy?) Will the keepers maintain some kind of professional cool in the face of this wondrous creature? Nope, I'm delighted to report. Their communications with Lucy are much more respectful than my cat-babbling but the affection in their voices is clear.

Something else I'm struck by: now that I've been allowed behind the scenes at the zoo I can't help but notice the parallels between this world and my own work environment. First of all, there is a stark contrast between the slightly grubby backstage area of the animal enclosures and the public displays, just as there is in the theatre, where the areas behind the beautifully appointed sets are often cramped, unattractive spaces. (Just to be clear, the state of these "backstage" areas at the zoo is entirely acceptable — think about any farm you've visited.) But it's also hard to escape the feeling that the animals on display are on stage, and that their homes — their "habitats" or "environments," never "cages" — are decorated sets. Complete with props. This gives me some great ideas about the point of view of one of my characters, who is able to step outside of the situation and see the zoo as a rather surreal performance of captivity.

Finally, it must be said: the zoo stinks. The smell of manure is not quite overwhelming but certainly ever-present. Perfectly understandable, and you really do get used to it, but it gives me an idea for a line for one of my characters, an unsympathetic type who is out of her element at the zoo, exclaiming about the smell.

NOVEMBER 19

My second shift: I show up to work with two keepers who are taking care of bunnies, frogs, and a few birds. One of the young women is training the other on handling these animals. She's a bit brusque with me — perhaps not all that pleased with being saddled with a civilian — but the trainee is pleasant and talkative. The zoo's veterinarian, a striking Quebecois woman, comes to check on one of the frogs.

Since I'm meant to function in much the same way as one of the zoo's volunteers on these shifts, I always ask if I can help with something. Today I'm given the job of ripping up paper for a parrot to play with. But I'll soon learn that if my offer of help on these shifts is accepted, it is almost always going to involve shovelling manure. It's a fact of zoo life that a good portion of the keepers' time is spent cleaning animal enclosures. I do marvel, more than once, at the fact that the keepers, many of whom have advanced science degrees, spend at least part of every day wielding a shovel.

Later in the shift, I go to see the zoo's collection of harbour seals. One of the keepers here is cutting up herring for the seals to eat, another is orchestrating a training session featuring a giant ball. The slick, shiny seals are extremely cute, with lots of personality on display. A strong impression I'm getting early on in this gig (which will be confirmed throughout my tenure), is that all the animals have distinctive personalities and that the keepers are completely tuned in to their individual qualities.

After I've stowed my steel-toed boots for the day, I go back to the administrative office to make notes. While I'm there one of the keepers from my morning session turns up in the office with Rosie, a serval cat, on a leash. (She looks quite a lot like a giant, wild version one of my pets, a moody tabby called Billy Bob.) I learn that animals which can be handled in this way are referred to as "tractable." When I comment on the fact that this woman has popped up in another role with a different species, I also learn that most of the keepers here are extremely versatile. While they might have some special skill or interest related to one species, they're expected to be able to work in many different areas with many different creatures. I suspect this is partly a function of the size of the zoo—relatively small—perhaps they can't afford to have staff unique to each species.

Today I start my shift working with a pleasant and cheerful woman (Della), who describes herself as a zoo "lifer." Her primary responsibility is running the commissary, where the food for the animals is prepared. The menu for this incredibly diverse animal population includes everything from produce to wee frozen rodents. Many of the animals also eat nutritional pellets which look dull but likely do the job. The zoo seeks out donations from grocery stores to supplement the demand for relatively expensive fresh food. I don't want to inquire too closely about the provenance of the dead mice.

My job is to cut up bananas and carrots into bite-sized pieces. Once the food is ready, Della and I go to feed the lemurs, and I experience the pure and simple pleasure of holding up a tray of food to each of these beautiful bushy-tailed creatures in turn, like a waiter at a cocktail party. (Almost all of them select bananas rather than carrots.) I'm thrilled to be a few inches away as they reach for the food with tiny little hands.

The next stop is observing as the vet gives a shot of medicine to a mountain sheep, assisted by two keepers. The sheep is in a small corral but still manages to partly scale a wall (reminding me of the choreography in *Crouching Tiger, Hidden Dragon*), as he attempts to escape. I then go off with one of the keepers to feed a snow leopard who is in quarantine. The zoo has a couple of areas where they can isolate sick animals or animals who have been on loan to another zoo and need to be certified as healthy.

I'm discovering that the urge to anthropomorphize these animals is completely irresistible. Officially, the zoo staff is meant to be caring and professional but maintain a sort of detachment. I don't even try. I'm respectful of the zoo animals' status as wild animals — I'm certainly clear on the distinction between my tabby and the serval cat — but I can't help but ascribe human emotions to them. Or even restrain myself from tiny foolish indulgences like referring to the lemurs' "tiny hands" rather than paws. This impulse is particularly powerful in relation to the elephant. There is nothing about this animal's appearance that invites comparison to humans but they are so intelligent — and emotional — that of course we assume they're like us. (And somehow that makes them more worthy of respect?)

The general public's affection for — obsession with — elephants means that many of us have some basic knowledge about them. Most people are aware of elephant poaching and have heard at least one account of elephants grieving a loved one. This general awareness of elephants may also include the knowledge that they normally travel in large family groupings. This is one of the main contentions of the activists who protest Lucy's presence at the zoo; she's on her own, with no other representatives from her species. (I try and fail to imagine what it would be like to be the only human in an animal world, forced to live in a burrow and endure well-meaning but clumsy endearments from a squirrel?) What's it like for Lucy to be on her own here, with only humans to love (if that's indeed how she feels), and be loved by?

The zoo did have a second elephant for a time, who left for a breeding loan in 2007 and never returned. From all reports these two did not get along and "Samantha" was apparently quite bad-tempered. But the mere fact of this other elephant's existence, on top of my research about the emotional intelligence of elephants, gives me the idea that perhaps the elephant in my play could be grieving the recent death of her only elephant companion.

One of the elephant keepers I consulted argued that whatever feelings an elephant might seem to be expressing (after the death or departure of the other elephant at the zoo) were probably just caused by suddenly having "less stimulation." After that I worry for a while that maybe I'm projecting some kind of fanciful layer of human feeling onto this splendid creature. But I continue to research and I find that the majority of experts in this field do indeed recognize the complexity of animal emotions.

Turns out zoo animals are often treated for depression or anxiety. For example, a polar bear at the Calgary Zoo was once medicated with Prozac in order to deal with his endless pacing.

DECEMBER 15

Today's shift is spent with an interpreter, a young woman whose job, among other things, seems to be roaming the site looking for children she can instruct and entertain. She tells me a bit about her background and gives me a tour of the reptiles, amphibians, and little furry mammals who are all housed in the same building. I learn that a group of meerkats is called a mob. (I am so endlessly delighted by these names for groups of animals.) These appealing little creatures have a complicated social structure, with sentries, hunters, and babysitters always on duty.

She also takes me to the room where she keeps educational props, including an elephant tooth and a pair of contraband cowboy boots, made from some restricted animal's skin (likely seized by Canada Customs), and various other artifacts. These objects are used to generate discussion about poaching and animal conservation.

We wander around for a bit trying to find an audience. It's a cold, weekday, winter morning so the zoo isn't exactly overrun by visitors. We finally meet an older couple and their six-year-old grandson. That's when the interpreter's talents kick in. She has a great manner, deploying gentle humour and clear explanations to engage this shy little guy. She gets a ball python snake out of its enclosure and encourages the little boy to touch it. He does, very tentatively, but with an expression so clearly awestruck that I don't doubt the impact of this encounter. His grandfather is thrilled; he confides in me that the little boy has never before been "brave enough" to touch one of the animals on their previous visits to the zoo.

Observing this simple encounter speaks to one of my big questions. One of the oft-repeated arguments for the existence of zoos, besides their conservation efforts, is to educate. David Hancocks, author of *Animals and Architecture*, expresses the argument this way: "We'll only protect what we love and we'll only love what we know." On the other hand, Rob Laidlaw, of Zoocheck (an organization that campaigns for the protection of wild animals), contends that there is no empirical evidence that people are educated at zoos. And indeed, this desire to educate the public can go terribly wrong. When the public was allowed to touch cownose rays as they swam past in a tank at the Calgary Zoo, more than forty of the fish subsequently died due to a lack of dissolved oxygen in their tank.

Based on what I witnessed today, I'd say the hands-on experience with that snake made quite an impression but I must confess I don't know if the awe and adrenaline experienced by this kid translates into anything useful in terms of his character development or in the formation of his values. I hope so.

However, this shift with the interpreter and hearing a bit about the zoo's educational mandate makes me wonder about something else. It's been suggested more than once by various anti-zoo activists that most people would benefit just as much from watching a great animal documentary on the Discovery Channel, with David Attenborough narrating in plummy, sonorous tones. And, furthermore, that the documentary experience is superior because you're seeing the animals in the wild, rather than in the artificial environment of the zoo. This argument has particular resonance right now. At the time of writing this, we're still in the midst of a worldwide pandemic, during which many of our interactions have moved online. Discussing the difference in impact between live and virtual meetings has become a familiar part of the public discourse. Does the experience of liveness have a substantially different impact? Is it more thrilling (educational?) to watch world-class photography of an apex predator chasing prey across the savannah than it is to have the tactile experience of touching a snake? I don't know. But it seems to me that one of the aims of the zoo, certainly manifest in the encounter I witnessed, is to create empathy. Do we get that same powerful, ineffable feeling when we watch a documentary? If we can't even begin to imagine the life of a snake or a bunny or an elephant — and of course we'll probably relate this to human experience — then why would we care if yet another species has been wiped out?

Toward the end of my shift with the interpreter we go to the Elephant House (still trawling for kids?) and witness some startling behaviour. As we enter the building, I catch a blur of movement out of the corner of my eye. One of the keepers who works with Lucy runs from the main area of her home to another room, then calls out. Lucy appears (from stage right), and *runs* from the other side of her house to find the keeper. They're playing hide and seek! I'm so used to Lucy being characterized as old and sick that it's a surprise—and a delight—to see her having fun. I'm reminded of the stories I heard from one of her original keepers. When Lucy was much younger she proved to be a brilliant escape artist, once making it as far as nearby Laurier Park. The police were called and when Lucy's trainer turned up the terrified officers were standing on top of their cruiser. She may not have the energy or means to escape anymore but by all accounts, she's still mischievous. And she obviously still likes to "play."

Writers are often asked to create character "bios." I normally spend a long time working on character backgrounds before I begin a play, and certainly when I teach writing I ask students to find a way to investigate their characters before leaping into the first draft. I've never tried to create a bio for an animal, but I find myself constantly comparing my imagined elephant with Lucy. I've decided that my elephant will be from Sri Lanka (rather than Thailand) and that she's still young enough—and healthy enough—to trumpet loudly. (Lucy has respiratory problems so she mostly just makes a kind of huffing noise.)

And oh, the naming—this choice of what to call a character always feels incredibly important. You're endowing them with a lifetime of associations (including the symbolism of the name), and challenges (irritating nicknames). I'm fascinated to discover that Lucy actually has two names: one for the public, and one for her keepers to use. This is mostly so that the animal in question isn't distracted from the commands of zoo staff by visitors calling out her name. I love the idea that my elephant has a private name, known only by her closest companion, the keeper. I search for an Asian name that has resonance and find a word that means "magnificent creature." That feels exactly right.

DECEMBER 17

Today I receive the list of all the animals at the zoo I requested a few days before. I go through the listing that night and find myself enthralled with the poetry of the names of species: capybara, chinchilla, fennec fox, Jamaican fruit bat, Sichuan takin, bearded dragon, blue-tongued skink...

JANUARY 6, 2016

After a Christmas break I'm back at the zoo. I'm so aware of the cold (around −20°C), that I can't help but wonder how the animals stand it. While the zoo has a respectable collection of North American animals (Arctic wolves, owls and reindeer, among others), and plans to expand this part of the collection in coming years, it's also home to many creatures from temperate zones. Most notably: Lucy. The image of this magnificent creature who could be pulling mangoes off trees and bathing in warm mud, instead living alone surrounded by concrete, in a cold northern climate is...challenging. But here she is.

Today is a Lucy shift, as it happens, so I'm excited about spending concentrated time with her and her keepers. We start in the large Quonset hut (roughly the size of a barn) built especially for Lucy's benefit so she can exercise comfortably in the winter. (Though it's not particularly warm in here and one of the keepers mentions that heat has been an ongoing issue.) I hover around the edges of the activity: two keepers playing ball with Lucy. She can kick the ball or toss it with her trunk.

There's a third keeper present, someone I've heard a lot about — apparently some of the staff call her Mother

Earth—but whom I've never met until today. She's been with Lucy (and at the zoo) for longer than anyone else currently on staff. It may be my imagination, but she doesn't seem all that keen to have me there and I guess I don't blame her. But I'm kind of desperate to get her perspective on Lucy so I try to be the right kind of presence— respectful and non-threatening but curious. I ask a couple of questions about the keepers' relationships with the elephant. Turns out Mother Earth used to be Lucy's primary caregiver, but Lucy really seemed to suffer if her beloved keeper took more than a day off, moping and refusing to eat. The zoo staff realized they needed to train more keepers who could establish a connection and work with the elephant.

At one point Mother Earth steps to a side door, cracks it open and lights a cigarette. I sidle up and start a conversation about smoking, confessing that more than twenty years after quitting, I still like the smell of "fresh" smoke. She reports that the younger staff at the zoo ride her pretty hard about her habit. "Gotta quit," she says, and nods toward Lucy. "I promised her I wouldn't die before her."

I get goosebumps. This is a confirmation of everything I'd imagined about the relationship between the elephant and the keeper in my play.

JANUARY 7

This may be the day when I have to prove my mettle and try not to show how nervous I am around our winged friends. (Love the sight of a waxwing at the bird feeder, hate the feeling of birds flying at or around my head.) I'm not phobic, exactly, but this is not my preferred species.

I'm shadowing Jim today, one of the older keepers, who has a deep knowledge of and affection for birds. We get into a golf cart and feed trays of dead mice and baby chicks to the "raptors" (hawks, eagles, owls). He explains the backstory of one of the zoo's senior residents, a bald eagle which has only one wing and would surely be dead if it weren't at the zoo. Jim talks about his own efforts to rescue and foster birds. Many of the keepers foster animals in their homes.

Our next stop is the nocturnal animal enclosure, a kind of murky cave which houses sloths and bats, among other things. I don't think Jim would have minded if I had declined the pleasure of being in this dimly lit, creepy enclosure, but I'm determined to seem plucky. In truth there isn't much for me to do. Jim takes care of the cleaning and also attaches fruit to the walls for the bats to eat. I'm standing off to one side by a large artificial tree when I catch a hint of movement out of the corner of my eye. I freeze — something (someone?) on the other side of the tree is on the move. Very, very slowly. It's like watching a picture develop, waiting for this object to resolve itself into an outline and then an identifiable face. It's a two-toed sloth. He slowly lowers himself off the branch, upside down, and then rotates his head toward me. He's curious. I'm so struck by the way the outside world disappears when we stare into each other's eyes. I return to the sensation again and again that day.

JANUARY 9

Any day that begins with Lucy is pretty much guaranteed to be fantastic. I'm shadowing Peter today, who is one of the several keepers who is allowed to work with the elephant. We start the shift cleaning up Lucy's main area, then it's time for the elephant spa. Three keepers gather around Lucy to give her a bath, soaping her up and scrubbing with long-handled brushes. Lucy then takes the hose and sprays herself, before taking a drink directly from the hose. Once the bath is done, one of the keepers prepares pails with warm water and Epsom salts, for soaking Lucy's feet. Elephants often have problems with their feet and Lucy's no exception.

Of course I'm not participating in any of these activities as anything more than an observer. I hang out and engage the keepers in conversation whenever it seems appropriate. This is partly just my human need to ingratiate myself with these people. But I'm also testing my theory that keepers may prefer the company of animals to humans. In fact, there seems to be a range of personalities doing this job. I'm particularly struck by one of the young men, trained to work with Lucy, who is a real talker—friendly, open, extroverted—the complete opposite of the keeper-type I had in mind. Note to self: don't generalize about the sort of person who works at a zoo. That said, Mother Earth seems to be very close to my literary version of a keeper.

Paul and I leave Lucy luxuriating in the attention—she'll get a kind of chiropodist treatment after the foot soak—and move on to feeding the quarantined animals: an eagle, little ponies, goats, an emu, and Hope the camel. I help clean up poop in the pony corral. Oh, the glamour...

Normally I spend my lunch breaks in the staff room with the keepers as I don't want to miss a chance to listen to them chat. But one day I go to a different lunch room, frequented more by office staff than keepers, and note that there's a poster with a photo of a "known activist" on the wall. Probably connected to some of the stories I've heard about Lucy's caregivers being threatened.

One of the pledges I've made to myself about my participation in this project is that I will seek out the activists who work tirelessly to bring attention to Lucy's situation. As I understand it, there are a couple of different factions in the Free Lucy campaign. The activist depicted in the poster is from a fairly aggressive group not above employing the odd guerilla tactic. More recently, another group has emerged on the scene with the same objectives but using different strategies.

The WWPT facilitates an introduction to this second group: LEAP (Lucy's Edmonton Advocates' Project). Deciding that the rather aggressive tactics of the other Lucy advocates don't seem to be working—and may in fact be alienating the wrong people—this group has taken a more positive approach. They produce pamphlets and beautiful children's books that argue for Lucy's freedom and they seem to spend a lot of time "tabling" at farmers markets and other such public events, getting the word out about Lucy's plight. These are smart, sensitive, reasonable people who are willing to spend countless volunteer hours reaching out to the public about this issue. They don't trust the veterinarian report that claims Lucy wouldn't survive the trip to a sanctuary. They want an independent review of her health.

Though I am thoroughly impressed by this group, there is one red flag in our conversation. I think I've been quite clear that I'm writing a fiction, not an essay arguing for the release of Lucy, but a few of the group's remarks imply that I could (and should) use the play to argue on Lucy's behalf. I don't think too much of it at the time, because I feel—or hope—that ultimately they'll understand my role as a storyteller. This assumption will come back to haunt me later.

That said, the passionate advocacy for the elephant is not only an important aspect of the real story of Lucy but also an important element in my play. One possibility is to create a character who is an activist and include him or her in the play's cast, which, at least in the early drafts, has only three characters: a fundraiser, a security guard, and the elephant keeper. I'm reluctant to add another actor, partly because of the additional cost to the production. (As a Canadian playwright one tries to give producers fewer reasons to say no to a play.) I decide instead to represent the activists as offstage characters. (Meaning: their presence is felt, talked about, and has an impact on the story, but we won't actually see them.) In the world of my play, the leader of their group is inspired by the more aggressive faction of Lucy activists. The fact of the matter is, although I respect and admire LEAP's more positive approach, there is more dramatic potential in depicting a different kind of activist. And certainly I'm not inventing them — they exist.

One of my many anxieties about taking on this subject is I find myself wanting to represent all sides of the argument about zoos. I want to be fair. And yet, as I keep reminding myself, the play is not a documentary. It's not an exposé or essay. What, then, are my obligations? To try to tell the best story I can about a subject I care about. To be true to the characters I have researched and created. And by that I mean, once the characters have taken shape and I feel I've captured their essence, I try to have them act authentically within that context. In other words, they can't just be mouth-pieces for a particular point of view. That said, I do think about character function. What is beginning to evolve in my play is a central conflict between the elephant keeper and the zoo. So my choices in terms of the other characters need to help amplify and clarify that conflict.

JANUARY 13

I'm excited about doing a "night shift." I turn up mid-afternoon, a little short of time, and rush through the experience of choosing my steel-toed rubber boots from the shelves in the staff area. Once I set out to join my keeper (Neela) for the shift, I realize the boots are uncomfortably small. (I don't know how I managed to make such a stupid, painful mistake.) I'm to join Neela at the quarantine area, which is a small building surrounded by a fenced-in yard. I wait for twenty minutes or so and realize I must have misunderstood something about the meeting. Eventually I locate the *other* quarantine area, a small building housing Goeldi's monkeys, some skunks, and a few meerkats. I meet Neela and the volunteer who's helping her; we set to work scrubbing the floors.

Once the grunt work is complete, the volunteer and I are tasked with making a "room" for the skunks, using branches from a spruce tree. The zoo solicits donations of discarded Christmas trees at this time of year as their fragrance and texture are appealing to many different species. I ask about the monkeys and hear from Neela that while the breeding program has been a big success, the monkeys aren't likely to be returned to their home in South America as much of their habitat there has been destroyed. So while the little room with artificial trees and food dispensers is no substitute for the Brazilian rain forest, it will have to do for now.

I discover that the meerkats are here for a respite from the bullying they've experienced from the rest of the meerkat mob. Neela points out that animals are perfectly capable of cruel behaviour: cannibalism, murder, genocide. They may be differently motivated than the human variety schoolyard tough, with some kind of biological imperative powering their behaviour rather than malice. But the outcome is the same. It's good to be reminded that wild animals aren't just soft and fuzzy models for Gund toys.

The volunteer leaves after helping in this first location and I'm left to do the night rounds with Neela. The routine is to check in on all of the animals on the site, to make sure everyone is accounted for and, in some cases, lay in an evening meal or a snack.

I love the way Neela talks to the animals; her tone is soothing and affectionate as she greets them or bids them good night. When we go to the other quarantine area, she brings the goats in from their little yard and asks them not to bully Daphne the sheep. One of them almost seems to bow his head in shame. Neela is fairly frank in expressing her opinions about the zoo. As we stop to visit one of the owls, perched high in an outdoor enclosure, she notes that because of the night lights at the zoo, the owls never get to have the deep darkness they crave. For some reason this makes me terribly sad.

We go indoors and visit Julia, the white-handed gibbon. I ask about some of the single animals at the zoo, as I'm discovering that Lucy isn't the only animal who is alone. Apparently when the animals are too old to breed, like Julia, the zoo won't bring in companions for them. Julia looks sad and mopey to me. I'm well aware that I'm projecting human emotions onto her, but I can't seem to help myself. I'm also struck by the fact that she never gets any fresh air.

We bring the wallabies in from outside and visit the other animals in the building. I didn't realize how many of the animals at the zoo are actually abandoned or confiscated pets. This isn't exactly the kind of conservation effort one thinks of in connection with zoos, but it's a real element of life here.

I'm given the task of counting the meerkats, who are piled on top of one another in a long tube. Except for the appointed sentry who watches my every move. Then we go out into the night again.

We check in on the Siberian tigers, who are eating meatballs and seem to stare balefully at us through the bars of their cage. They have a large yard but this enclosure is where they get their meals. And then on to visit Lucy. Neela gives her more hay and some food in a bucket. We visit the Arctic wolves — gorgeous white beasts ghosting around their enclosure — and then to the farthest reaches of the zoo to check on the "hoof stock." It's eerie to be the only two people (apart from a security guard, I assume), wandering this peculiar community of wild creatures, bidding them good night. I wonder what the long winter darkness feels like to them — endless? I remind myself that animals have a completely different sense of time than humans.

I know now that I want to show my security guard character doing his rounds at night. I like the idea of him communing with the animals when there is no one else on the site. It feels both lonely and peaceful. The former emotion aligns with his situation — he's a grad student from Rwanda, still suffering from vestiges of PTSD, who talks about the animals with his dead brother and is particularly focused on the Siberian tigers. He may also be the right character to question the idea of quality of life as it relates to both wild animals and humans. Is it always better to be alive than dead, no matter what quality of life one has?

I continue to be surprised, moved and inspired by some of the things these keepers say to me (or in my presence). Although ultimately the script I write is a blueprint for many other artists (directors, actors, designers) to amplify and influence with their own choices, at this point all I have is dialogue to tell the story. And the lines of dialogue that leap out at me from these precious encounters at the zoo are not merely one side of an exchange in a dramatic scene. In some cases that one line opens up a whole world of feeling. As in: "I promised Lucy I wouldn't die before her."

Now that I have a clear view of the keeper character, I wonder more and more how to characterize the elephant in the play. I work hard at articulating the right actions and emotions for my human characters, expressed in their text and subtext, but I'm at a loss as to how to reflect the elephant's inner state. The elephant's communication, while not necessarily realistic, has to be shown in some way that makes emotional sense. A talking elephant might be terrific in a children's story or a musical but I'm aiming for something different.

Years ago, when I first became interested in this story, I read an article in the local newspaper about an activist group's efforts to put Lucy's situation in front of the courts. (The legal challenge was unsuccessful.) One of the activists quoted in the article said "Who speaks for Lucy?"

This simple question haunts me throughout the creation of the play. My elephant keeper (Karen) wants to speak for the elephant (Matara) but she also agonizes about getting it right. She used to feel that she could communicate with her beloved charge, but Matara has fallen silent. She really does want to know: if Matara could speak, what would she say? I really wanted to know, too.

JANUARY 17

This Sunday morning I do a shift with Gary, one of several smart, good-humoured young guys who work at the zoo. He makes me laugh right off the bat when he says he has pets:

a turtle and a cat who "help each other get into the garbage." This shift also features one of my favorite animal encounters. I get Gary to snap a few photos of me crouched by a capybara, a very large rodent, native to South America. When, years later, I hear about someone eating capybara, I actually cringe with revulsion. Maybe I'll turn vegetarian yet.

One of things I'm investigating while I'm here is the communication between keepers and the animals. I've read quite a lot about animal empaths as part of my research and have already interviewed someone who claims to have psychic connections with wild animals. It's not something I ask all the keepers I shadow but I get the feeling that Gary might be receptive to the idea. He is. He says there are no words in his communication with animals but sometimes he feels like he can make them "appear." He backs up this notion with several anecdotes.

I also quiz him a bit about my keeper personality theory and he expands my understanding of the "types" who love this job. He claims that the bug experts may look and act a little "Goth." And that "bird people" are the weirdest. He also makes a statement about animal activists that really strikes me, saying he supports their existence and even many of their actions as they pressure the zoo to do things they really should be doing anyway.

The fact that these issues are so complex is enlightening, and also useful for constructing the dramatic arguments in the play. There is no black and white judgement to be made. It's not a matter of right and wrong; it may be, as a playwriting colleague of mine once said about an ideal dramatic premise, a matter of *two* rights—equally powerful forces vying for the audience's sympathy. This situation is rife with that kind of complication.

JANUARY 29

Zoo School: The zoo runs regular programming for school children and today I'm going to tag along. I pull into the parking lot just as a bunch of Grade 2 students are piling out of school buses, forming lines at the entrance gate.

Once we're all inside, the zoo employee running the show today takes the kids through an exercise of identifying animal artifacts, then asks them to draw pictures inspired by this experience. Viewing Lucy is next on the agenda. The kids are prepped — "Lucy's a bit tired so be quiet" — then lined up for an orderly entrance into the Elephant House.

The kids are awestruck by the sight of the elephant and ask lots of questions about her behaviour and her early life in an elephant orphanage. I'm really interested in what the kids actually think about Lucy's presence here. What's the impact of seeing wild animals in cages? Hard to tell, though one little girl leans over to an adult (one of the parent helpers), and says: "Lucy looks so sad. Is she sad?" Unfortunately I can't make out the adult's answer without making it too obvious that I'm eavesdropping. Lucy does a couple of manoeuvers, responding to cues from the keepers, and gets a popsicle as a reward.

The kids are then dispersed to various outside areas to observe animals and start on a composition. I do my best to help out, coaching some little boys on words they might use to describe the Arctic wolf. As I'm doing that a group of junior high kids amble by — teasing, laughing, jeering, all the standard, mostly harmless, adolescent badinage — but then a couple of them decide to howl at the wolves. I can't tell if this has an impact on the wolves but it seems cruel. It occurs to me that my over-protective elephant keeper would be enraged by behaviour like this if it were directed at the elephant.

FEBRUARY 2

I suit up for another chilly winter shift and join a keeper (Mary) and a volunteer on their way to the "big cats." First up: the Siberian tigers.

We scrub the floors and watch the vet examine a gash on the back of one of the tiger's legs after luring her into a secure holding area. Once that's done and both tigers are locked inside, we go outside to the tigers' yard, which has many landscaping features and several old Christmas trees. I'm given two ampoules of Chanel N°5, donated by Holt Renfrew, and told to spray a little on each of the trees. The tigers love the smell, apparently, and they also love sniffing pieces of fabric that have been scented by being in the meerkats' enclosure.

Chanel N°5: this is a reference I've used in the play in a line from the fundraiser character ranting about the smell of the zoo. It seems a bit magical that this comes up during the shift, though I realize it's a tiny detail. But it won't be the first time I discover some convergence between what I've written and reality at the zoo.

After Mary feeds giant meatballs to the tigers we move on to the lynx, which she is training to put its feet up on the fence, using a device that emits a little beeping noise. We check in on the blind snow leopard—someone else who would most certainly be dead in the wild—and say hello to Rosie the serval cat.

The visit to the Arctic fox is an exercise in patience. We wait for quite a long time (in silence) for Bianca to emerge from hiding. She stares right at me, then the volunteer, then finally snatches a frozen mouse from Mary's hand and goes off to eat it.

Another magical convergence comes up when I meet with the zoo's fundraiser later that day. She's describing the impact of the zoo on visitors (like the little boy who donates his birthday money to them every year). She tells me another story about an international student, studying engineering at the University of Alberta, who used to visit the zoo regularly; he particularly loved the Siberian tigers. After his untimely death his parents came to the zoo because they wanted to see the animals that had meant so much to their son. I'm stunned — this is essentially the story of my security guard character: an international student studying engineering, who particularly loves the Siberian tigers. Maybe these notions just drop down out of the ether...?

FEBRUARY 4

Today I'm paired with a young man called Timothy. Like many of the other keepers, when asked about best and worst aspects of this job, he says the very worst thing is the death of one of the animals. Devastating. And the best thing, for Timothy, is talking to the public about his work. We hop into a half-ton truck to go to the farthest reaches of the zoo to take care of the "hoof stock."

I get to feed Buddy the camel and help to clean up his enclosure. We check on the bighorn sheep, Sichuan takin, and finally the Eurasian Tundra reindeer, who are all named after Nordic gods.

Timothy lures the reindeer herd into a field adjoining their enclosure, where they cavort and high-leap in a manner worthy of the Bolshoi, while we shovel poop and rake hay in their main corral. After finishing this I'm meant to follow the keeper into the barn but I decide instead to schlep one more shovel of dirty hay to the garbage bin. When I return from this task I am confronted by "Freya," a lone reindeer who has wandered back from her frolicking. She head-butts the shovel out of my hands — I find out later she likely wanted to rub her antlers against the wooden handle — and then just keeps coming. I don't know how else to stop her except to grab her antlers with my red-mittened hands. I wrestle with her for three or four surreal seconds before it occurs to me to call out for help. The keeper is there in an instant. Phew. And wow.

Several weeks later the short plays we've been asked to write as a part of the WWPT project are presented to the public. I deliberately chose not to write about the characters in my full-length play, instead writing a monologue for a zoo keeper doing a night shift. The zoo staff as well as the activists are invited to attend. (Part of the point of this initiative is to bring new or non-traditional audiences to the theatre.) My contact from LEAP is unable to attend but she sends a couple of colleagues to use her tickets. They report to her that they were angry and disappointed by the point of view in my piece, and that there "was nothing about the animals." Not true — the keeper character speaks lovingly of the animals and critically about the zoo — but I guess we sometimes see what we want to see. I get a tersely-worded email from LEAP along with a request to see the script. It feels like the end of our cordial relationship. I realize that no matter what I write, in this short piece or the full-length play, perhaps nothing short of a full-out condemnation of the zoo will satisfy them. I'm a little sad but maybe there was never any other possible outcome.

In the fall of 2018, my play *Matara* has its premiere at Workshop West Playwrights Theatre. It's the end of a very long creative journey — I don't think I've ever worked harder on a play in my life. Overall the premiere is a huge success, with great press and wonderful audience response.

The theatre also hosts post-show discussions dealing with animal issues after several of the performances, and I'm thrilled by the passionate interest expressed in these forums.

It's now nearly five years since my residency at the zoo. Going over my notes for this essay, many moments come back with sharp clarity, perhaps because they were imprinted with adrenaline or awe. I still have no answers to my own questions about zoos. My bottom line — the quiet horror of seeing wild animals confined — has never changed. And although I really don't think it's feasible to move Lucy at this point — many experts believe she wouldn't survive the trip — I sincerely wish she'd never been in the zoo in the first place. (Or, if she were destined for captivity, that she was at a wildlife park with other elephants.) That said, if she'd been left in Thailand her fate might have been a lifetime of hauling logs. It's complicated.

In December, 2020 Jane Goodall calls on the zoo to transport Lucy to an elephant preserve in Tennessee — another high-profile protest added to a long list that includes Bob Barker and William Shatner. Closer to home, I read about an Edmonton woman who has recently taken it upon herself to mount a weekly — solitary — protest at the zoo, calling for Lucy's release. She says in her interview with local media that the decision was made after years of visiting Lucy, accompanying school groups as a teaching assistant. On one of those visits she looked deep into Lucy's eyes and felt like Lucy looked back. And that…was it.

ACKNOWLEDGEMENTS

Matara was developed with the assistance of countless artists who participated in workshops and readings at Workshop West Playwrights Theatre, Urban Stages, Skirtsafire Festival, and Script Salon. The play also benefitted greatly from a residency at Edmonton's Valley Zoo (facilitated by Workshop West Playwrights Theatre and the Edmonton Community Foundation), and the incredible generosity of the staff there. I gratefully acknowledge these contributions as well as the support of the Canada Council for the Arts and the Edmonton Arts Council. Finally, special thanks to Tracy Carroll, who was part of the journey from the beginning.

PLAYOGRAPHY (*Selected Productions*)

Fresh Hell – Shadow Theatre, 2023

Oh! Christmas Tree – Roxy Performance Series, Theatre Network, 2018

Matara – Workshop West Playwrights Theatre, 2018

Pants On Fire (The Mommy Monologues) – Skirtsafire Festival, 2017

Night Shift (This Is Yeg) – Workshop West Theatre, 2016

The Invention Of Romance – Workshop West Theatre, 2014 (Published by Playwrights Canada Press, Toronto, 2016)

Oh! Christmas Tree – Lunchbox Theatre, 2012

Terminus – Horizon Stage, 2012

Jake And The Kid – Theatre Calgary, 2009

Ooga Booga – Concrete Theatre, 2008 (Published by Playwrights Canada Press, "Sprouts Anthology of New Plays," Toronto, 2010)

The Myth Of Summer – Alberta Theatre Projects, 2005 (Published by Playwrights Canada Press, Toronto, 2008)

The Aberhart Summer – Citadel Theatre/Alberta Theatre Projects, 1999 (Published by NeWest Press, Edmonton, 1999)

Homesick – Workshop West Theatre, 2000 (Published by Playwrights Canada Press, Toronto, 2008)

Sky Geezers – Alberta Theatre Projects, 1992

Dustsluts – Workshop West Theatre, 1992

Gravel Run – Alberta Theatre Projects, 1988 (Published by Blizzard Publishing, Saskatoon, 1991)

CONNI MASSING is an award-winning writer working in theatre, film and television. She is a graduate of the University of Alberta, where she earned an MFA in Playwriting, and has lived in Edmonton ever since. Recent stage credits include *Matara* and *The Invention of Romance,* both premiered by Workshop West Playwrights Theatre, *Oh! Christmas Tree* (Roxy Performance Series), and her widely produced stage adaptations of W.O Mitchell's *Jake and the Kid* and Bruce Allen Powe's *The Aberhart Summer.* Conni has worked as a writer and story editor on television series such as *Mentors, The Beat, North of 60, The Adventures of Shirley Holmes, Taking it Off* and *Family Restaurant.* Film projects include *Invisible,* co-written with and directed by Neil Grahn, and *Voila,* directed by Geraldine Carr. Her published work includes six plays and a full-length comic memoir, *Roadtripping: On the Move with the Buffalo Gals,* as well as short fiction and non-fiction for various magazines and journals. Conni's writing has been recognized by the Betty Mitchell Awards, the Elizabeth Sterling Haynes Awards, the Alberta Film and Television Awards, the Academy of Cinema and Television, the Writers Guild of Alberta, the Writers Guild of Canada, the EAC Artists Trust Fund Award, and the Alberta Playwrights Network Playwriting Contest. Conni is a proud member of the Playwrights Guild of Canada, the Writers Guild of Canada, and a founding member of the Alberta Playwrights Network.